Smart Selling!

Your Roadmap to Becoming a Top Performer

Tom Butler

Published by The Lawrence Group LLC
P.O. Box 10478, Sedona, Arizona 86339

ISBN 0-9772169-0-X

Library of Congress Control Number 2005932329

Printed and bound in the United States of America
by Sheridan Books, Inc.
Ann Arbor, Michigan 48103

Cover Design, Artwork & Layout by Artline Graphics, Sedona, AZ
Edited by Mary Ranjana Blackett
Edited by Bob Kelly, WordCrafters, Inc.
Manuscript Assistant Margo Gravesen
Webdesign & Hosting by IamIsee Multimedia, Las Vegas, NV
Front Cover Photo by Dreamstime

DEDICATION

A special thanks to Ernie Bencivenga, Jeff Saul and Bill Hymes, remarkable people who gave generously of their time and refused to allow me to wear out their patience, try as I did.

And finally, to those good souls who have attempted to teach me the art of writing and storytelling...that is still a work in progress, I hope I can repay the kindness!

CONTENTS

Introduction

Have you concluded that learning to sell products and services is important to your own personal and business success? You have already taken the difficult first step. How you learn to sell still remains your true challenge. In the real business world, most learning happens through costly trial-and-error exercises or sporadic education. Remember, every day you struggle as a salesperson, or an entrepreneur, costs you precious time and money. Failing until you learn to get it right, or are forced to give up, is hardly a solution! Besides, that approach could waste several years of your time.

This book has three primary audiences: first, students about to discover the challenge of an early career sales assignment. Many recent graduates are working in sales because it's both a testing ground for talent and often the only entry-level position available. The second audience is composed of experienced businessmen and women who are undertaking the need to sell for the first time. The last group of readers are the entrepreneurs who have started, or now own, a business that needs to increase sales performance.

Most importantly, I do not assume that you come to this book with much sales knowledge or experience. I'm going to give you a simple, yet effective, approach to understanding and then mastering the selling challenge. The quicker you put our information to work in your daily business life, the sooner you'll reap the benefits.

If you own or work for a business that sells products or services to other businesses, this book is a clear roadmap to reach your goal of becoming a top sales performer. While some of the concepts explored here are applicable to the challenge of selling in the retail arena, the current curriculum of Smart Selling! focuses on business-to-business selling.

I started my own sales career with a handshake from my new employer and his best wishes! My training was in real time in front of prospects. It took me several years to figure out it was possible to cause success rather than hope for success. This vexing reality occurs countless times every business week. My job is to help you avoid this dilemma.

You'll start by learning both fundamental selling skills and a repeatable customer-oriented selling methodology you can put to work now! We'll teach you what to do, how to do it, and why it's important at each step of the selling cycle, stressing communication skills and delivering the right message to the correct audience. You will quickly discover what the top sales professionals understand about achieving sustainable success without the pain of a lengthy learning experience!

Chapter 1 introduces **The Four Selling Profiles**. There are four basic types of salespeople. The key characteristics of each profile can help you decide which sales jobs will work best.

The Essence of Selling reveals the fundamental skills of selling that every practitioner must master, including key insights into communication skills that can quickly accelerate your performance.

Chapter 3, **The Selling Pyramid**, answers the question: "To whom do I sell? What message should I deliver?" You'll learn to maximize the limited selling time you have and to minimize time spent with people who cannot purchase your product or service.

The Business Sales Methodology is a step-by-step, business-to-business sales process which gives you Goals/Actions/Results to execute at each point of the sales cycle. It will become your roadmap to closing business.

Chapter 5 introduces you to **Forecasting Your Sales Results**, a troublesome business challenge whether you're a business owner or a salesperson. We will teach you how to integrate forecasting with our sales methodology. This chapter provides you with a complete set of usable forecasting forms.

Chapter 6 defines **The Ten Personal Skills of Top Performers**. These important skills set top performers apart from the ordinary! Once you understand their importance, I believe your own results will quickly improve.

The key actions in **How to Get and Keep Your First Sales Job** and, better yet, succeed at the assignment, are described in our final chapter.

Journey through these learning experiences and become a better sales practitioner. Then, call upon this book time and again as you gain experience and face new challenges. Thanks for allowing me the opportunity to advance you into the ranks of Top Sales Performers!

Enjoy the book and the smart selling to follow!

CHAPTER 1

The Four
Selling Profiles

Where do you fit?

Roadmap Notes

To Salespeople

The profiles will serve as a reminder of the two essential issues—not all sales positions will be an ideal match for each selling personality; both the action axis and change/risk axis serve as benchmarks to enhancing your performance. It is important to find opportunities that work with your profile.

To Managers

You maximize the effectiveness of your sales team when you are able to match sales personalities to sales assignments.

To Business Owners

Turnover in a salesforce is both expensive and disruptive. Salespeople who underperform or fail are often mismatched to the position they hold. We help you get the right people in the right assignments.

The Salesperson Profiles

What type of salesperson are you? Understanding where you fit in our Four Selling Profiles will allow you to decide what type of selling assignment best suits your strengths. The profiles give you invaluable insights to learning important selling skills, achieving personal growth and reaching your goal of becoming a top performer. If you are driven and committed to be in sales, then you will want to be a top performer.

Makes and exceeds assigned quotas

Sets the pace for the entire team

Consistently achieves plan

TOP PERFORMER

FINISH

Working in the wrong selling assignment can make your arrival at top performer status more difficult than it has to be and diminish your enjoyment of the career choice you have made.

There are no "free passes" given to any profile when it comes to the fundamentals. Every profile demands that your selling skills be fully developed and applied to each prospect or customer.

The profiles have been created to give you the opportunity to reflect on how you deal with two very fundamental challenges: the ability to accept change/risk and the willingness to engage in action-oriented tasks. It is important to remember that there is no correct "Profile" and you can rise within any category to top professional status if you are in a sales assignment that accommodates your profile. Very few salespeople will fit at the maximum level of any profile. The use of an axis suggests that there will be gradients within each category.

The Profile Axis

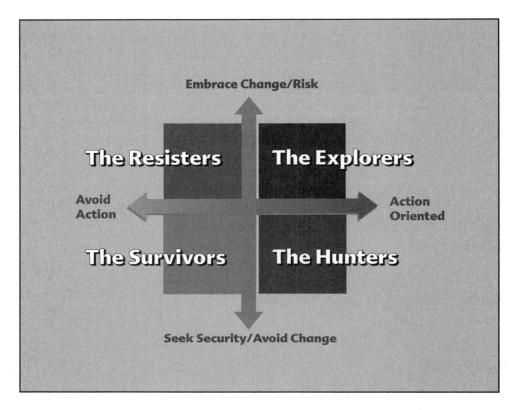

Shortly, we will have a discussion about *The Essence of Selling*. We will conclude that setting goals, taking actions and getting results in a continuum are the core of every selling assignment. Underlying *The Essence of Selling* is the Profile Axis we have created, which is built on:

- The Action Continuum
- The Change/Risk Continuum

Selling is about action, and each of us embraces action in a different way. Some act first and think later. Others will procrastinate and delay taking action on any and every issue in both life and business. We each have a natural comfort zone where we seek to live when it comes to action. Understanding our comfort zone, and consciously evaluating if we need to remind ourselves to accelerate or to restrain our actions, is a challenge many top performers have learned to manage. In my selling experience, I have learned it is valuable for me personally to slow down my natural tendency to act quickly. Being hyperactive did not always allow me to set goals or get the results I wanted.

Change is all around and a constant in our lives. The business environment of the 21st century is marked by ever increasing degrees of change that will accelerate in the foreseeable future. Some people embrace change and truly enjoy and seek out new experiences. Other individuals are uncomfortable with change and will go to great lengths to avoid or minimize this exposure whenever possible. The companion of change is risk. Accept change and you accept risk.

Selling assignments can range from repetitive and predictable to unique and exploratory.

How you view change will have a significant impact on how comfortable you will be in a particular sales role. I have known numerous successful salespeople who recount: "My last sales job was very regimented and I didn't enjoy the experience, despite my achievements." Others will claim, "The assignment was not very well defined and I wasn't comfortable in the unstructured environment, even though my sales record was excellent."

The point I want to stress is that you can become a top performer regardless of your profile, if you remember:

- The need for action and the response to change are always present in any sales position.

- Managing the alignment of your sales assignment to your personal selling profile will increase your chances of success. Conversely, taking an assignment that is at odds with your profile will make your ability to reach top performer status more challenging.

- Your commitment to enhancing your sales skills and developing the personal attributes that lead to success must be ongoing.

In effect, you can savor the wisdom of 10 years of selling experience, or repeat the mistakes of your first year of selling for the next 10 years.

The Explorers

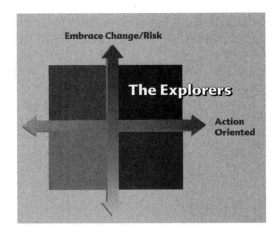

Explorers are driven in their pursuit of their goals. They are change-oriented and highly action-oriented. They often stand out quickly in selling organizations because they are so energetic. A strong action impulse leads them to embrace more prospecting activities and engage new opportunities on a continual basis. Business owners and sales management like the energy Explorers bring to their assignments. They may or may not deliver results, but they sure are given credit for trying. The comfort they display with change often leads them to explore new sales niches that may not be currently in their company's mainstream marketplaces. They will appear to many peers to be oblivious to fear and willing to undertake risk. They are viewed as natural leaders.

Explorers become top performers when they develop selling skills to complement their ability to accept change and undertake action. Early in their careers, they can resemble "misguided missiles," percolating lots of activity with very little focused direction, wasting time and energy on poorly qualified suspects and market opportunities. Learning the fundamental skills, disciplines and a methodology to manage a selling assignment is critical for Explorers. They are often bright and quickly grasp the fundamentals of selling. Those who struggle usually fail to commit to the learning experience, relying instead on being energetic for whatever success they achieve.

Explorers must undertake challenging selling positions because they are oriented to accepting and undertaking change. They will quickly lose interest in highly structured assignments, including products and services that appeal to mature or late-stage marketplaces. Explorers are entrepreneurial and will gravitate to those types of business. They will make statements such as, "Give me a new product or idea and let me figure out where or how I can sell this solution." "Anybody can sell toasters. I want to sell molecular nanobots to a yet-to-be discovered marketplace."

Explorers will often accept highly leveraged compensation arrangements. During my own recruiting and hiring of sales representatives, the Explorers displayed an appetite for risk and accepted sales plans that included a modest base salary but a very strong commission incentive. Remember, they are driven to success and have a confidence that allows them to accept risk in return for extraordinary rewards. I have also observed these Explorers quickly reason that if they are not successful at a particular assignment, they'll move on to the next lucrative opportunity—here again, their comfort with change shows through. They have little problem accepting and acting on changes in business conditions, reorganizations or other factors. Just be aware that they also have little difficulty jumping ship to a new challenge/opportunity when they lose confidence in their current employer or their own business.

Explorers' Preferred Sales Assignment:
- **A selling challenge which includes introducing a new product or concept to a marketplace.**
- **New business ventures.**
- **Sales assignments that require penetrating new marketplaces with established products.**
- **Markets and products that may be incomplete or undefined.**
- **Assignments with minimal amounts of infrastructure and support.**

The Hunters

The Explorer profile is often compared with a Hunter. It is true the incumbents of either of these profiles are strongly action-oriented. The single most distinguishing difference is the desire for security and tolerance of risk. Let's consider American history of the early 1800s as an analogy. Meriwether Lewis and William Clark were true Explorers. They discovered new frontiers 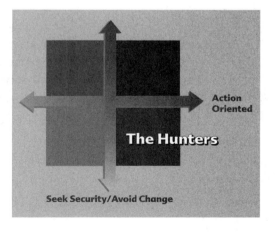 and set their eyes on uncharted rivers, lands and natural wonders that were truly unknown to their contemporaries. Later, across 19th century America, in contrast, countless frontiersmen ventured into the wilderness territories to hunt and farm—the brave men and women who turned raw land into prosperous towns and cities sought and created the security of communities that rarely interested the Explorers.

Hunters are hard working, energetic and dedicated. The ranks of top professionals are heavily populated with Hunters. You will find them selling products and services from early life cycle to mature offerings. Many Hunters will have long periods of employment with the companies for which they sell (or own). They are committed to their business, and it's important for them to play a role in making sure the companies are successful. This attitude is an extension of their natural desire to be secure in their sales assignments and the business where they work.

They may struggle when given new selling assignments, and keeping a successful status quo will have real appeal to them. They need careful assurances and communication about reorganizations or changes to new business conditions. When confronted with deteriorating marketplaces or declining product life cycles, their first reaction will be to work their territory or assignment harder than they had in the past. The dedication will be commendable and security seeking.

Sales compensation plans that include competitive base salaries will matter. Commission incentives will be viewed as important, but they place priority on the security of a predictable base salary. Raising the base pay of a Hunter will be viewed very positively; an Explorer will care more about an increase in the commission rate.

Hunters' Preferred Sales Assignment:
- **Selling well-defined products to a marketplace that is beyond early-stage volatility and risk.**
- **A stable support structure with modest amounts of assistance.**
- **A company or business with a predictable environment.**

The Resisters

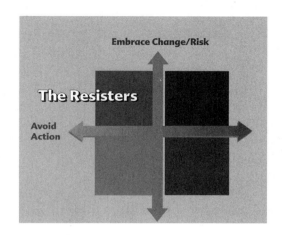

Salespeople who fit the profile of Resisters are a challenge and potential jewels. They are conflicted in their ability to accept change and then act. This personality profile can be best summarized by a wise old adage: Actions speak louder than words.

The Resisters can intellectualize change. They will verbalize the need for it and espouse accepting it, so they can be confused with Explorers, but Resisters struggle with taking action. Two habits are often indicative:

- First, a failure to act is often blamed on managers, co-workers and outside events, for example, "I couldn't make this call because I lacked the appropriate marketing material," or, "Our presentation is inadequate." Acting when beyond a zone of comfort is difficult for a Resister. Explorers will face these same issues and just continue to sell or act to fix the problems themselves.

- Second, Resisters avoid what really needs to be done by actively spending selling time doing projects, working on committees or assignments that are not going to result in making sales calls, prospecting or closing business.

"Sally was a very popular and well-liked salesperson. She was always willing to give generously of her time to help the marketing team, or work with engineering on suggestions to enhance our products. She was always available to offer her opinions about how the company should and could do better. Her sales performance was marginal, but we were all reminded that her territory was not the best, and we did not really give her all the management or product support she needed to do a professional job. When we appointed one of her peers to become her direct sales manager, she was very upset. Bob, who was very hands on, delivered a simple message: No more distractions, take responsibility for your own success, forget the excuses, and get on with selling new business or leave the sales team! Within several months, Sally had begun to dramatically improve her sales performance."

Executives and sales managers who are selling products or services in volatile, unstable and uncharted markets will discover those who are the Resisters on their selling teams; unfortunately, the discovery may come after months or years of quandary. You will hear statements such as:

> *"Jeff was one of our best sales representatives, but when we targeted a new market for our product he never quite reached his past levels of performance. I know he understands we have to sell in a different way, it just seems he is struggling with his activity levels and adjusting to our new targets!"*

Newly hired salespeople who seem to be change-oriented in an interview sometimes fail to display that appetite for action once they're hired. Why?

> *"John came into our company, professing a desire to be part of a new business going through enormous internal challenges and trying to sign customers in a new market. He had all the right answers about how to deal with and sell in a volatile environment, yet he seems unable to deliver real results."*

Sound familiar?

Resisters can easily be top performers if they discover and embrace the need to focus on action, rather than procrastination or avoidance. Managers who demand action when hesitation begins to creep into the sales process can inspire and impact real performance.

For many executives and small business owners, the worst hiring errors occur from miscasting Resisters as Explorers. I learned from experience to be careful with successful candidates coming from large, stable selling environments who profess an interest in risk-intensive selling positions.

Resisters' Preferred Sales Assignment:
- **A well-defined and positioned product sold into markets that are also well-defined.**
- **A strong infrastructure and sales support system.**
- **A management team actively involved and participating closely with the sales force.**

The Survivors

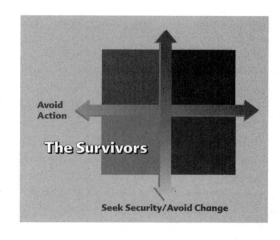

The question is always asked, "How can someone who has a problem with change and is not action oriented possibly survive in sales?" Should this personality profile be encouraged to go into sales? The simple answer is yes. Survivors can succeed at sales *if* they are given the correct selling assignment and *if* they willingly work at stretching their comfort zone. In fact, they can flourish in the right environment.

This personality comes into a sales assignment wanting to do nothing more than survive. Many will tell you they had deep reservations about selling and really believe they marginally fit in a selling environment. In truth, many will quickly opt out of sales and seek other assignments, some of which are peripheral to the selling organization. Others stay in sales because they become comfortable with surviving in a known environment, rather than risk change. Do not underestimate Survivors. They can grow as a result of the confidence that comes from experiencing success and the desire to be Top Performers.

Survivors become accomplished sales professionals when they are placed in assignments that are narrow in scope and very predictable. These assignments may include selling existing clientele additional solutions that build on the value of a product they already own. In addition, Survivors can sell commodity products or services that compete on price or delivery arrangements that are closely controlled and managed by their company.

In addition to being an author, I operate a small publishing business. We receive numerous telephone sales calls from our suppliers. The salespeople are often inexperienced and typically working their first sales assignment. Recently, I reordered some promotional brochures. The saleswoman who manages our account was eager to quickly complete the order. However, once I began asking about changing color specifications on the brochures, the level of her confidence diminished. She was clearly nervous about what to do next, "I'm not sure how to change any specifications. It's not a request I've had before and I don't want to make a mess of the order!" I assured her I was sympathetic to her challenge and

19

that change was just a part of being in sales. "Speak with your supervisor and call me back when you have some answers to my request." I suggested she consider having their graphic designer available for our next call. Several hours later, the same account manager called to brief me on her progress and her plan to meet my new specifications. She had clearly regained her self–confidence. We agreed to a conference call with her graphics department and supervisor. The order was processed the next business day and the results were flawless! Could our salesperson have managed a complex competitive sale or challenging new business call? Not at this stage in her career! Inside sales or telemarketing is often a great learning environment for Survivors.

Survivors need to stretch the envelope of their comfort zone. First, they need to recognize their profile and then work to absorb and accept change in small increments. They need to constantly remind themselves of their need to act on selling tasks, rather than the more natural state of waiting and procrastinating. They may never achieve the comfort Explorers and Hunters find in the selling experience, but they can grow and experience success.

Survivors' Preferred Sales Assignment:
- **A very regimented and controlled sales environment.**
- **Well-defined scripts and lots of management oversight.**
- **Product must be specific and well-targeted to predictable markets.**

Once you have identified how you currently fit in the "Selling Profiles," you are ready to begin! Explore and learn the basic selling skills and personal skills that will allow you to become a Top Sales Performer.

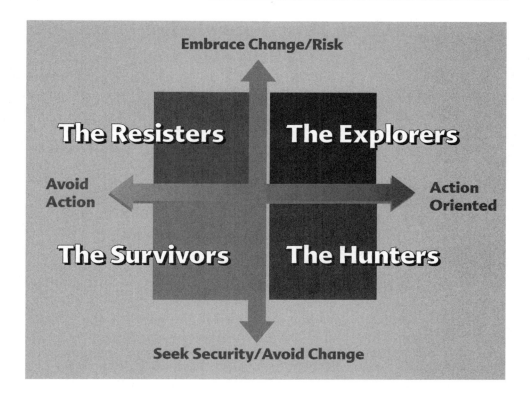

Final Reminders!

The Four Selling Profiles will help you reflect on the importance of selecting sales positions that are aligned with your current personal profile. Choosing the correct position allows you to both maximize the enjoyment you will experience in your vocation and advance your ability to achieve top performance. Sales assignments, much like people, are often unique and distinctive—no one size fits all!

There is also no single profile that is exclusive to top sales performers. In fact, as you grow, mature and evolve, the profile that you best fit now will change to reflect the new you! Perhaps you will remain a Hunter but embrace change with more comfort than you were able to in the past. A Resister may evolve into an Explorer by learning to act without hesitancy. Today's Explorers may seek more security and evolve into Hunters.

The profiles also serve to remind each reader that embracing change/risk and a commitment to being action oriented represent opportunity and challenge for all sales practitioners.

Test Your Knowledge

The Four Selling Profiles

1. How many selling profiles have we identified? _____

2. Explorers are always the best salespeople.   True/False

3. What is the Profile Axis built on?
    A. Persistence and Intelligence
    B. Extroverted and Fearless
    C. Action Continuum and Change/Risk Continuum
    D. None of the above

4. Your current profile will never change.   True/False

5. The Explorer needs to be challenged in the sales
    assignment and should avoid selling mundane
    products in mature markets.   True/False

6. Hunters seek _____ in sales assignments.

7. Resisters can best be described as:
    A. People who struggle with "Actions speak louder than words."
    B. Have difficulty with change.
    C. Require sales positions which feature security and supervision
    D. All of the above

8. Survivors can achieve success in sales if they are
    placed in the correct job.   True/False

9. Very few people are a pure match to any profile.   True/False

10. Why is it beneficial to understand where you fit in the
    profiles?
    A. It gives insight into what jobs best meet your needs.
    B. It is always interesting to analyze yourself.
    C. It may help you negotiate an employment package.
    D. It allows you to reflect on how you embrace change/risk.

CHAPTER 2

The Essence of Selling

Fundamental Skills for Successful Business-to-Business Selling

Roadmap Notes

To Salespeople

The Essence of Selling is your roadmap to developing a predictable, measurable and efficient way to manage your prospects and customers. The number one cause of failure and under-performance in selling is the lack of a game plan. The top performers in your profession do not succeed because they are lucky or even personable. They succeed because they understand and embrace the principles that are the basic building blocks of *The Essence of Selling*.

To Managers

You will succeed or fail in your assignment in a direct correlation to the performance of your sales team. Your job in many ways is simple: make the salespeople who work for you successful. Allow them to achieve and exceed expectations. Leading them to achievement starts with assuming nothing. *The Essence of Selling* lays out the fundamental skills and tasks that drive ongoing sales performance.

To Business Owners

The success of your business starts with a healthy "Top Line." Your sales team is integral to delivering new customers, expanding relationships with existing customers, contributing to customer satisfaction and creating a positive perception of your company. The challenge you and your sales management team face is making sure the sales staff understand the core nature of their assignment. *The Essence of Selling* clearly communicates the key tasks and skills necessary to create sales success.

The Essence of Selling

The Essence of Selling is our roadmap to understanding the sales assignment and succeeding. Some of us embrace sales because we cannot envision a more rewarding career; others come with reluctance, and some arrive with true fear and anxiety. However you have arrived in sales, the ultimate challenge is always the same: How do I succeed as a salesperson? How do I deliver results quickly and make a real contribution? In time, you will begin to ask how do I get better at selling? What do I have to learn, correct, avoid, or change to really achieve and sustain success?

The first rule of successful selling is simple:
**   SALES DO NOT JUST HAPPEN!**
Failure to understand this single principle is the cause of most unsuccessful sales assignments and careers!

The failure rate and disappointing performance experienced in this profession is higher than necessary because the field contains very little training. It is beset with too many motivational speeches augmented with advice focusing on various selling tips and tricks. Motivation and sales tactics are important; but they are not, by themselves, a foundation upon which to build successful performance.

My own observation after 25 years of selling is that top sales performance is not an exclusive domain reserved for a select group of gifted individuals. The fundamental skills that drive extraordinary performance can be learned. Years of costly trial-and-error mistakes are also avoidable.

I have heard countless vice presidents of Sales complain bitterly about sales representatives who were supposed to be experienced professionals chosen on a resume showing years of experience and wisdom, but lacking the fundamental skills to achieve a sales quota. The executives also lament the long start-up times that inexperienced sales staff and newly-minted sales representatives go through before they can become productive members of a selling team. From the subordinate side, I have listened to hundreds of these same salesmen argue that they were never trained or told what was really expected of them. The irony is that everybody is partially correct.

25

What really matters is that you develop and embrace a repeatable game plan that is consistent and measurable - one that allows you to deliver results.

After countless sales calls and sales meetings over a 25-year period, at home in North America and around the globe, watching interactions between customers, prospects and salespeople (some successful and others just plain failures), I started to explore the foundation of selling. It seemed logical that if you could understand and learn the basic activities of successful selling, then you could begin to refine and replicate success. I quickly realized that selling is not a single act, but a series of interactions between buyer, seller and a community of interested parties to the transaction. It's a continuum of activity! The three core activities of the continuum fell into place one at a time.

Goals-Actions-Results

Selling begins with the setting of **GOALS.** What is a goal? The dictionary defines a goal as, *"the purpose toward which an endeavor is directed; an objective."* There are two types of goals:

Strategic goals are big picture plans we want to achieve...the dreams we want to turn into reality, for example, "Selling a flagship product to the Major World Corporation," or achieving 200 percent of my annual sales quota!

Tactical goals are specific in nature requiring attention to execution. Without execution they are nothing. The phrase, "The devil's in the details," is an excellent reminder—ignore the details, forget about executing tactical goals, and you are set up to fail! Securing an introductory meeting with an important prospect or deciding how to persuade an administrative assistant to put your important telephone call through to the "Chief" are tactical endeavors.

The top sales performers understand that the big picture *strategic* goals matter; but detailed planning and execution of each *tactical* goal is paramount! You must continuously create, set and reset your goals throughout your sales process. Every prospect interaction results in new goals. In effect, we are constantly moving to our next step, our next objective.

Goals lead to the second step in our selling continuum... **ACTIONS!** Selling, by its very nature, is an action-oriented task. Without action you cannot achieve the goals you are constantly setting. Each goal you set leads you to the next action you have to undertake. Actions include communicating with prospects, doing presentations, objection handling, asking for orders, and countless other tasks.

RESULTS!...The third activity in our continuum of selling is about measurable results. Without results, you have nothing. Much like goals, results are both *tactical* and *strategic* and are attained continuously throughout the sales process.

The *Essence of Selling* requires setting deliberate GOALS, taking specific ACTIONS and getting measurable RESULTS in a continuum for each account you have or are attempting to create.

We can easily test *The Essence of Selling* by asking one simple question! If I fail to set goals, take action and get results, will it matter? Well...I think the answer is both intuitive and clear. You may succeed in spite of yourself, but I sure wouldn't like to bet on your chances for long term, sustainable achievement.

Each day at thousands of businesses, salespeople show up for work and flounder by failing to embrace and act upon the fundamental skills of selling. They do not fail on purpose, but they are guilty of not taking the time to ask what is at the core of successful selling. Many are also guilty of falling into the trap of believing that "sales just happen." Their managers are just as guilty. My experience is that they often communicate a message that says, "Look, I pay you to sell! So, go sell and quit making excuses!"

Let's take an example from the world of professional sports. Do you suppose professional football players would show up on a Sunday morning, sit in a locker room, put on their uniforms and then ask each other, "What team are we playing this week? What are we supposed to do to win this game?" Not very likely! They will study films of their next opponent from dawn to dusk each weekday, practice plays they believe will work, and even script their game plan play-by-play. The coaches work alongside their players each and every day, just as hard, to orchestrate a victory!

Sound familiar? In sales, we call this *The Essence of Selling*.

The Process

A sales process provides the discipline, which allows you to develop a repeatable game plan to manage your prospects, benchmark your progress, and monitor the results you want to achieve. In fact, without a selling process, you really have no way of controlling your interaction with customers and prospects

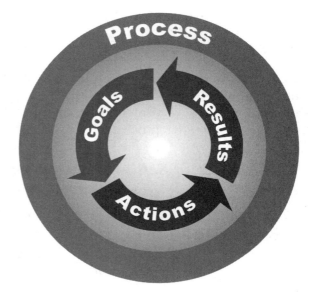

The word "process" makes many salespeople squirm. What you hear goes like this: "Process is what management uses to interrogate me! It's the source of countless reporting assignments that prevent me from spending time doing real selling! The more information I reveal, the more questions I get asked! Process is my prescribed pipeline and forecast, right?" Unfortunately, what many companies call process is really an internally focused administrative or reporting system that is used to manage the sales team.

Do not confuse management's internal requirement to obtain information with your need as a salesperson to have a working process for selling that is externally focused on suspects, prospects and customers.

If your company does not have a documented sales process for the product or solution you are responsible for selling, one of your first challenges is to develop your own process. I know a number of top professionals who became accustomed to working in business environments that had very little in the way of a defined sales process.

Entrepreneurial companies are replete with countless examples of little to non-existent infrastructure. At other companies, the message is that they just want the sales team to get results: "We know it's difficult to manage, but we just want results. How they get those results is up to them."

This dilemma goes to the core of the frustration many salespeople experience and voice: "No one told me what to do!" This challenge applies equally to seasoned as well as brand new sales personnel. In actuality, a good measure of the real problem lies in the manner of selecting and training sales management. If your sales management team never used a prospect-centered process when they sold, or if they come from outside the sales arena, it is highly probable that a defined external selling process does not exist. You need a prospect-centered sales process regardless of your company's internal operational environment. Any process, even one that is incomplete or flawed, is better than no process.

Here is a preview of the process we have developed—The Business Sales Methodology—which gives you a precise step-by-step roadmap that can be implemented in any business selling assignment. The complete BSM will be presented in Chapter 4.

The Business Sales Methodology

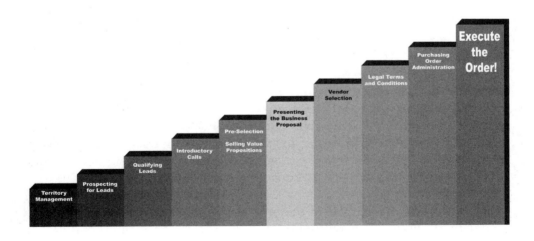

Communications

The ability to communicate is the final element of *The Essence of Selling.* The dictionary defines communications as, *"the ability to express oneself in such a way that one is readily and clearly understood."* Sounds simple enough, but we all know it's an incredibly difficult challenge. Sales are inextricably tied to communications, and the best salespeople have developed a set of communications skills that advance their effectiveness. We are going to explore some of the big payoff communication skills that will make a real difference, quickly, to your selling efforts.

I can remember my mother saying to me as a teenager, "Bobby really likes to talk, you just cannot stop him once he gets going. He is going to be a great salesman." It was her way of encouraging a shy teenager to speak up, but it also reflected a cultural bias that equated salesmanship with talking.

Here is our first powerful communications insight: the act of talking is not, by itself, communications. It is part of communicating and a part of the selling equation, important, but not the Holy Grail of success. For years, I've observed salespeople talking past prospects and talking themselves out of opportunities, while spewing out facts, figures and technical jargon no one cares about except themselves.

Once, while observing a call with a new colleague, I recall kicking his foot under the table to get his attention after failing in several polite attempts to interrupt his presentation. He had subjected this rather important customer to a 20-minute lecture on our product's very detailed specifications. The prospect, a very senior executive officer, was completely disinterested in this level of specifics with good reason! He had a very large and expensive team of technical experts. It was apparent that he was not very happy, and was about to ask us to leave his office. My colleague, barely skipping a beat, turned to me and said, "Please stop kicking my foot, it's breaking my concentration!" and proceeded on for another five minutes. He was mystified when the prospect interrupted his speech to announce that he was out of time, got up and left us sitting in his conference room. Worse yet, this sales representative was upset that he never got to finish his presentation. "I haven't finished telling him about the product." You can guess what my reaction was!

Every act of sales communication should accomplish four objectives:
- ### Achieve the goal you set for the event
- ### Result in learning by both parties
- ### Help to build a relationship
- ### Reach agreement on the next step

Every act means telephone calls, face-to-face visits, any and all discourse with your prospect. Does this mean some of your communications will fail? You bet! However, once you get used to Setting Goals-Taking Actions-Getting Results, you will realize that both success and failure require you to reset the continuum of Goals-Actions-Results again.

In the world of sports, star baseball players hit .300. That means they fail 70 percent of the time they go to the plate. The hitting masters practice day in and day out. They also have been known to watch the videotape of each at-bat they have, successful or not, to learn from the experience before they come to the plate again. That is the continuum of Goals-Actions-Results in the purest form. I'm sure you can think of countless other examples.

Setting goals is integral to every act of sales communication.

Why are goals important? Simple—without goals you have chaotic action and sporadic results. In plain English, you flounder! When you flounder, you communicate to your prospect a lack of leadership. Make no mistake, prospects seek leadership qualities in the salespeople with whom they choose to do business. They demand affirmation that they are placing their company and their career in capable hands. I believe one of the most significant causes of failure in the sales assignment is the inability to set goals.

Does this story sound familiar? A sales manager and his salesrep are in the building lobby of a prospective account. The manager asks, "So, what is the plan with these people?" The salesperson responsible for the account replies, "Well, we are going to meet with them and see if they have any interest in our product." Happens every selling day in one form or another! In fact, it appeals to a sales mentality that is anxious to live on the edge. The theory goes that if you are smart and very glib, you will talk your way through the call into some form of success. The problem is compounded by management, which tolerates this behavior.

Let's replay this scenario a different way: The sales manager and salesperson in the lobby had thoroughly discussed events leading up to this sales call. They agreed upon the goals for the meeting and decided who was going to execute the actions necessary to achieve the desired results. Which team would communicate leadership to the prospect?

A sales call without a goal is a disaster waiting to happen...and it will!

As previously discussed, goals come in two categories: strategic and tactical. Strategic goals are the big picture – the plans we prepare for landing a prestige account, beating quota by 200 percent, gaining financial security and retiring at 50. They are important and motivate us to exceed beyond our expectations. I always tell sales folks, "If you can dream it, you can achieve it!" Why? Because I believe it is true! Tactical goals are where most of us struggle. These are the detailed plans that require cold hard execution. For example, my goal is to get a meeting with the "Chief" by next week. How do I execute this goal? If my plan is to get a document to a prospect that includes a detailed cost justification, how do I accomplish this? Tactical goals require actions and lead to tangible results.

Use our Sales Call Plan worksheet for every call, then after the call, grade yourself on how well you did. The worksheet is at the end of this chapter.

Selling forces you to learn the value of setting goals, and this is the reason so many successful CEOs and entrepreneurs started their careers in sales. I have observed consistently that as sales executives mature and experience real success, what you hear them discuss again and again is their goal setting. They learn to anticipate each move and countermove necessary to keep the selling process moving forward and on track.

All sales communication should result in learning by both parties.

32

How do we make sure we mutually learn from our communications? Two skills will take you a very long way: Learn to listen and learn to ask questions!

Let's start with several basic listening principles:
1st Concentrate on the speaker.
2nd Acknowledge your attention and empathy.
3rd Distinguish the "I must have" and "I need" statements from the "I would like" and "I will consider" declarations.
4th Body language matters in face-to-face meetings, as does etiquette on the telephone.

When you listen attentively to someone, you invite him or her to disclose, confide, and trust in you. There is no higher compliment than communicating that you value what the speaker has to say. The reverse is also true. How many times have you personally complained that, "No one listened to me?" Not listening breeds anger, frustration, mistrust and mistakes. Which set of emotions do you want your prospects to experience?

To concentrate on the speaker, you start by clearing your mind of countless other distractions. Remind yourself that in the time together, "I must make this person the focus of my undivided attention." The prospect may be disrupted by his or her own circumstances; but I have found that if I behave politely during the prospect's disruptions and continue to concentrate, the person will begin to respond to my concentration and reciprocate.

In face-to-face meetings, acknowledging your attention and conveying empathy starts with eye contact. If eye contact does not come easily to you, find someone with whom you are comfortable, a friend or relative, and role-play to practice making direct eye contact. Nod your head, or comment "I see...I understand...I agree, or...Excellent," to reinforce that you are paying attention and are interested in the speaker's thoughts. These same acknowledgements of attention are even more critical for successful telephone communication.

Discovering what the prospect "needs" and "must have" is critical for success. Would you buy a product or service from someone who never asks what you need or must have? Okay, you might buy a bottle of water on a hot Arizona day without asking! I suspect, however, that you would not spend your company's capital without having a complete discussion about what you need. Yet, the unfortunate truth is that far too many salespeople never uncover a clear understanding of the prospect's need. They instead focus on what they or their company have decided the prospect needs.

Here's a quick story from my own sales career. Fresh from product training and newly minted as a sales representative, I called on a CFO at a major bank to discuss my financial control system. I was very anxious and focused on making a good impression. I began with a quick introduction about my employer and launched into my trusty list of incredible product features. The crusty CFO stood up, waved his hands to stop me and said: *"This is what I need your product to do for me. Will it do that?"* When I replied that my solution clearly did what he needed it to do, he removed his glasses and sternly said, *"Tom, next time ask me what I need and save both of us a lot of time."* My first customer, and not an easy experience!

You sell your prospects what they need, not what you may want them to purchase! When I make this statement someone will occasionally ask, "What if our prospects do not know what they need?" Two comments: first, people who do not have a need don't buy very much. We call them suspects, not prospects. Our strategy, as a result of listening and asking questions, is to help them discover a need that may not have surfaced yet. The second most common scenario is that a real need exists, but they are not aware that a way to fulfill their need is available.

Body language and telephone etiquette...remember, the sole subject of our attention is the prospect. Start with good posture; I personally like to lean slightly forward into the conversation. Keep your body language open, avoid the fidgets, and do not cross your arms or use facial expressions that will communicate negativity, frustration or hostility. Turn off the cell phone or pager! Observe the prospect's body language—it will tell you a lot about the person's level of comfort with you, and receptiveness to the conversation.

Telephone etiquette starts with a "no interruption" rule. When I am on the phone with a prospect, I neither respond to the beeps for call waiting, nor do I ask prospects to hold while I see to some emergency or other disruption. Always ask before you use a speakerphone. Some people react negatively to their use, and I suspect they fear that other unannounced participants are listening to the conversation.

The art of asking questions starts with the big six: Who? What? When? Where? How? and Why?

Open-ended questions encourage an open dialogue. Asking questions leads to listening, listening leads to learning, learning leads to more questions and our communications are advanced. Another continuum! So, why is it that so many questions remain unanswered in the sales process? It was never lost on me that the top performers left only a few, if any, questions unanswered. In fact, I could often judge the chances of success for new recruits based on how many of my review questions they couldn't answer.

Asking questions can be a frightening experience for many of us. Why? The answers we get! Those answers expose us to a reality that may be unpleasant. We may be told we are not doing well, they like our competitor better, our solution is not a fit with their company's needs, or the prospect does not understand our message. Fear and Bad News!

In sales, you have to come to terms with the reality that what you DO NOT know can and will hurt you.

The only way to know reality is to ask, listen, test the response and ask again, until you are crystal clear about the answer. This is learning. Ask this question of your prospects at each and every opportunity you get: HOW AM I DOING? It will pay enormous communication dividends.

All sales communications should help to build relationships.

Attend any sales gathering and you will always hear salespeople talking about their commitment to building relationships or being relationship oriented. Why are relationships important? For some, it is a self-protective reflex to a cultural image of salespeople as charlatans and hustlers, a way of pronouncing, "I am different." For others, it is an excuse for being unable to move a sales process forward, asking for the order or taking a necessary but difficult action because "It will hurt my relationship." Relationships matter because, whether you sell to a small business, a large company or a global giant, the following fact remains unassailable:

A business is composed of people...and people buy from people!

Selling is business, and unfortunately, it is easy to confuse relationships with personal friendships. Having good relationships with customers and prospects is more than important, it's critical and mandatory. Relationships require mutual respect and a commitment by both parties to work to mutually agreed upon results. Prospects expect salespeople to sell, to ask for commitments and to close orders. Relationships will not be destroyed or damaged by doing your job – which is selling!

Let's explore the "people" with whom we communicate as sales practitioners on a daily basis. They are a unique and diverse group, but science has taught us that for all their disparity, they are remarkably alike. Remember the Human Genome Project? It discovered that humans are 99.9 percent genetically identical!

What Do Most People Want?

- **They want to be treated as "special."**
- **They want a better future.**
- **They desire direction.**
- **Their needs come first.**
- **They want to be successful.**

Every act of sales communication should result in reaching agreement on the next step.

Remind yourself to always close conversations, meetings, and even e-mails, with a suggestion for what is next! You may not always get concurrence on the first try, but your effort will succeed.

My very first sales manager taught me that selling is about providing others with something they value. Salespeople are the providers of value —value we deliver to our customers through products and services— products and services that meet their needs as individuals and business people. Value, like beauty, is in the eye of the beholder; to understand and appreciate it, people may need help.

Throughout this book we discuss three types of people in a sales audience. **Suspects** are people who may have a need for your product, but have yet to be qualified. They will often comment, "Tell me more!" or say they are willing to learn about your product. When they are qualified, they are called **prospects**. And finally, those prospects who have decided to purchase your product are called **customers**!

Final Reminders!

The Essence of Selling is the foundation on which success in sales is built. It is both the core discipline and repetitive methodology you will use to manage your prospects and customers as they examine and explore value. It is also a system to monitor and measure your performance. The Essence begins with three interlocking and continuous activities:

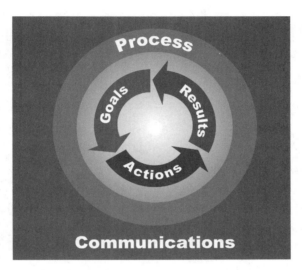

Setting Goals - Taking Actions
Achieving Measurable Results

Our Business Sales Methodology allows you to embrace a process you can repeat, monitor and measure. These three activities rest on the foundation of Communications. Without the skills to communicate value, no one will be able to effectively learn why your product or service is truly valuable...that is, unless you believe products sell themselves, which I do not!

All your sales communications must:
- **Achieve the goal you set for the event**
- **Result in learning by both parties**
- **Help to build a relationship**
- **Reach agreement on the next step.**

The Essence of Selling is a clear explanation of the sales assignment and the skills, disciplines and methodologies you must master in order to achieve the success you want.

THE SALES CALL PLAN

Call Date:..

Summary of the last activity at this account

....

....

....

Commitments I made

....

....

Commitments still outstanding

....

....

CALLING ON: Mr/Ms ....

Title ....Position in Selling Pyramid..................................

Current relationship with this Prospect

....

Positive Factors	Challenges
*	*
*	*
*	*

How do I build my relationship?

....

My Goal for this call

My understanding of the Prospect's Goal for this call

What do I want to learn from this Prospect?

What information will I share?

My Company

My Product

The Competition

My Business Proposal

What results do I want from this call?

What action will I ask the Prospect to commit to undertake?

Test Your Knowledge

The Essence Of Selling

1. The core of *The Essence of Selling* is
    A. Discover Prospects-Engage-Close Business
    B. Goals-Actions-Results
    C. Communications-Process-Leadership
    D. Strategy-Skills-Actions

2. Communications and Process are elements of
    The Essence of Selling.   True/False

3. The first rule of successful selling is:
    "Sales will just fall into your lap!"   True/False

4. Draw the depiction of *The Essence of Selling*

5. The two types of goals are   and

6. A sales process is important because it allows you to create a
    repetitive game plan to manage prospects.   True/False

7. List four objectives every sales communication should accomplish:

    _____   _____

    _____   _____

8. Making a sales call without a goal...
    A. Should go well.
    B. Is a disaster waiting to happen.
    C. Is the smart way to do business.
    D. None of the above.

9. Discovering what a prospect _____ is critical for success!

10. Top Performers sell prospects what they decide is best
    for the prospective client!   True/False

CHAPTER 3

The Selling Pyramid

Roadmap Notes

To Salespeople

Selling to the right audience, and understanding the inherent needs of that audience – these two skills are among the key differences between Top Performers and everybody else. We will show you who to sell to and what message they need to hear and why. Your real selling time will increase as a result of learning to avoid people who cannot make decisions.

To Managers

Increasing the performance of each and every member of your selling team is a key challenge. Making each salesperson both productive and successful starts with getting them to identify and call on the decision makers in their accounts. Just as important is teaching them that different needs exist at each level and position in a prospect account. Focus on meeting those needs and you greatly increase your selling power. *The Selling Pyramid* guides you to do exactly that!

To Business Owners

Salespeople are an important part of the public face of your business. They are also the primary channels to your "Top Line" sales performance. Having a sales team that delivers a consistent message about your company and products to the right audience is essential. Knowing they are interacting with the real decision makers for your customer and prospect accounts, and understanding what matters to those executives, advances the opportunity for successfully growing your business.

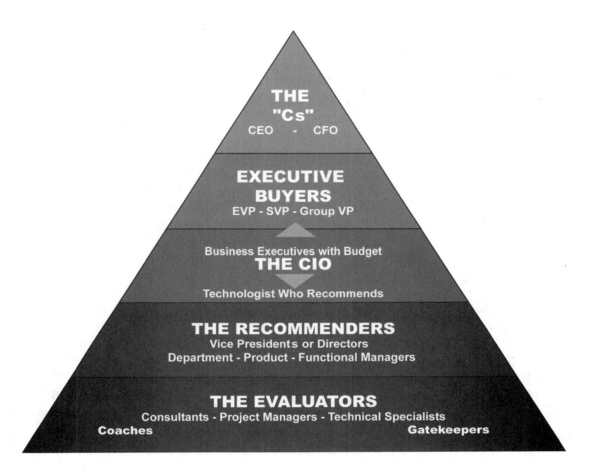

To whom should I sell?
What message do I deliver to that specific person?

These are the two powerful challenges that impact the sales performance of individual salespeople and, ultimately, the potential for growth of their company.

Have you ever calculated how much of your selling time is spent on people who cannot buy your product or service, even if they wanted to do that? How much effort is wasted on sales calls that result in, "Thanks for your time, we'll call you if we're interested." Selling time is finite, every wasted hour is an hour you cannot get back! Top performing salespeople understand that the foundation of sustainable success in sales is to whom you sell and what message you deliver.

What is The Selling Pyramid?
How will it accelerate my success as a salesperson?

The vast majority of business is organized in some form of hierarchy. For some time now, there has been a vigorous academic debate about the effectiveness of a hierarchy versus a collaborative team style. In fact, many companies are a blend of both approaches. However your prospect chooses to organize, I can assure you that you will universally find individuals assigned to the roles we are going to discuss within the selling pyramid. The roles in the pyramid, by definition, will require that the officeholder work to a distinct set of needs in order to contribute and prosper in his or her assignment.

CEOs will have different needs and wants than a Project Manager and you had better understand those differences before you meet with either —that is, if you want your meeting to be successful! Unfortunately, far too many salespeople waste valuable opportunities by failing to recognize and respond to this simple reality. This is not about manipulation, it is about responding to the real needs that matter to each officeholder. Fail to meet the needs of your prospects, and your selling effort fails!

In my time as a CEO, it never ceased to disappoint me that so many sales representatives insisted on telling me excruciating details about their product or service, despite my clear verbal statements that I was not personally qualified to judge those details nor interested in them. In fact, I would mention that I had a very competent group of executives who were both responsible for and interested in hearing those particular details. It was often clear that we were caught in a communication chasm —I was going to learn about product features they were instructed to talk about, rather than what I really needed and wanted to know. The bottom line: poor sales communications, a waste of everybody's time and money.

The Selling Pyramid is designed to help you understand the assignment of your audiences. It will assist you in focusing on meeting their needs when you communicate the value of your product or service.

You must sell to multiple levels in the Selling Pyramid. The wisdom is to engage each specific audience.

The Cs

The Chief Executive Officer, Chief Financial Officer and Chief Operating Officer are the most senior business executives. The larger your prospect's business, the more challenging it will be to get an appointment. However, these executives are not impossible to reach if you sell smart!

Many pundits will tell you that to sell successfully in today's hyper-competitive markets you must sell to Cs. The truth is—they are correct! What they don't tell you is that cold telephone calling, barrages of e-mails and snappy, clever headline letters have very low rates of success, if any at all. Many of those techniques were far more viable in the late 1990s when treasuries were overflowing and almost any new product and service solution could be in vogue.

Today, operating expenses have been slashed to the bone in most businesses, and no Chief has either the time or interest to spend precious corporate or personal resources responding to the dozens of promised miracles received each day. Executives have less capital to invest and they are more discriminating and cautious about using it. Doing business with peers and known vendors matters because it is viewed as both safe and prudent.

The best leverage to a meeting will come through senior executives in your own company. Why? Cs love to network. They understand the power of personal contacts, it's how the vast majority become Cs in the first place. Ask your CEO, or another very senior executive officer, to contact the Cs of the prospect and ask for a meeting. Trust me on this, there are very few CEOs who do not enjoy being asked. They will relish the opportunity to assist you, and the prospect's executives will respond to direct contact from your executives before they entertain calls from yet another unknown sales representative.

I have found industry pundits, well-known consultants, academics, attorneys or business community leaders to be great sources of introductions or referrals. Finally, you can often get an Executive Buyer at the prospect account to introduce you and your company's "C" to his or her "C." Introductions are important in a business environment that is under stress! Put your company's executives to work in the sales arena. The Cs are busy people. So, expect that your meeting will be relatively short. Once you get your audience, here is what matters:

They care about, and you must focus on:
1. **Profits**
2. **Increasing shareholder value**
3. **Growth of market share**
4. **Their employees' welfare**
5. **Their legacy, both public and personal**

How does our company and its product or service advance these needs?
Answer this question and you will have a successful meeting and greatly enhance your opportunity to add a new account. Unfortunately, the opposite is also true—a poor performance will hurt your selling efforts. I believe you do these meetings only to advance your campaign—failure is not an option.

What are the most common causes of failure?
- You did not focus on the five needs.
- You did not have clear GOALS for the meeting with an ACTION plan and expected RESULTS.
- You appeared to be disorganized or "just visiting."
- You failed to Listen, Ask, and Learn.
- Your solution did not add value to Cs needs.

The Chief Financial Officer (CFO) deserves a special mention in today's capital-restrained environments. He or she may well be empowered to manage any and all capital expenditures with an iron fist. You have to reach agreement with the CFO that your product is both valuable and meets whatever capital measurement criterion he or she employs. That means, you must understand the measurement hurdle and be prepared to address how your product will comply. The sooner you do this the better!

The Executive Buyer

The next power center on the Selling Pyramid is the Executive Buyer, with titles such as Executive Vice President, Senior Vice President or Group Vice President. They are responsible for major functional areas, such as Sales, Marketing, Engineering, Manufacturing or Operations. They also can have geographic or divisional authority. Most importantly, they personally make or control the final decisions on products and services because they own or control budgets and the funding of proposed expenditures.

Much like the Cs (to whom these Executive Buyers typically report), they also have a busy schedule and their focus on "What can you do to help me?" is very common. The vast majority of Executive Buyers aspire, publicly or privately, to be Cs. They are driven, well polished and political as they work to achieve their aspirations of success.

They care about, and you must focus on:
1. Growing revenues and/or their business unit profits
2. Reducing expenses
3. Increased productivity
4. Enhancing their career aspirations and image

How does our company and its product or service advance these needs?
The quicker salespeople find and engage the Executive Buyer, the more efficient and successful the selling efforts will become. Unfortunately, far too many of us avoid the very audience that can and will decide the fate of our proposal.

Three principles to remember:
1st   People buy from people!
2nd   A relationship with the top executives in your account is leverage you can bank on when you work with the Recommenders and Evaluators who are always present.
3rd   If you fail to engage the Executive Buyer, your competitor (who does) will have an enormous advantage!

The act of getting a meeting with this busy group of people is not easy, but it is manageable and done every business day. Top performing salespeople have learned to master this art with good reason. They understand it pays to communicate with Executive Buyers.

Marginally performing sales reps or the inexperienced will often fall into the trap of inventing or anointing Executive Buyers. The arguments will go like this: "John is the senior project manager for this evaluation. He is much more powerful than his position would indicate." Or "Jeanne will decide whether to buy or not; she is well connected in the company on a fast track."

My rule of thumb is simple: if your contact does not have a significant title or report directly to the Cs, the chances of him being an Executive Buyer are slim. In our example, John may well be an Evaluator or a Recommender, especially if he is focused on asking about product features. Test John by getting him to introduce you to his boss. If he or she turns out to be a middle level manager, I can assure you your Executive Buyer is still to be discovered!

A final note of encouragement: Executive Buyers are savvy business people. Salespeople with products that can meet the four needs they hold important will get the chance to present their solution. Remember what really matters to Executive Buyers and then ask for an opportunity to assist and engage them.

The CIO

The Chief Information Officer's assignment* comes in two basic forms:

- Business executives who have budget and funding authority. These are Executive Buyers.

- Second, technologists who recommend or certify acceptable solutions. They may manage systems architecture and infrastructure but the ability to budget and fund product decisions beyond their immediate department is outside their reach. These incumbents are Recommenders.

Caution is in order because the CIO may be an Executive Buyer for one specific set of products and a Recommender for another set.

Controversy has surrounded the CIO position, as evidenced by press coverage about the short 2- to 3-year tenure of most incumbents. Debates about why CIOs do not more frequently rise to the CEO position are common in the IT press. Some pundits have argued that the role of many incumbents is that of a mid-level member of the management team.

The bottom line, in my judgment, is that CIOs are important and worth engaging in your selling activity. They are generally knowledgeable, well connected in their own companies and often a product-friendly audience. Remember, a major part of their charter is to be well-versed in a wide spectrum of products and services. If they are not buyers, then they will advise the buyers. They can be excellent coaches and are a good source of references and new sales opportunities when they move to the next company or assignment.

Your first goal must be to determine if a CIO is an Executive Buyer or a Recommender for your specific product or service; then, focus on what he or she cares about!

The Recommenders

These people use your products and are directly affected by their impact. They will have such titles as Vice President, Director or Manager. They are responsible for managing divisions, departments or business units with specific functions: the Director of Customer Support, Vice President of Quality Control, Manager of Investor Relations. They are responsible for budgets but often will not have the final say on how, when, or if, the budget is to be used. I have found that this group will have more discretion when the economy is strong and their employers are meeting profit goals. They are among the first to be constrained when finances turn down.

They care about and you must focus on:
    1. Detailed product functions and features
    2. Department productivity
    3. Security and comforts

Understanding Recommenders really matters in your ability to communicate successfully. Here is the key point:

Recommenders cannot give you a final "Yes" but,
they can say "No" and sustain it!

This means you or a member of your selling team has to satisfy their need to ask questions and learn about the functions and features of your product. You do this by carrying through on the three objectives of *The Essence of Selling*, being certain that every sales communication with this audience:
- Achieves the goal you set for the event.
- Results in learning by both parties.
- Helps to build a relationship.
- Reaches agreement on the next step.

49

When you focus on Executive Buyers and their needs, this does not mean you ignore the Recommenders and their needs.

Several years ago, I had a chance meeting with a very senior Executive Buyer of a long-standing customer in a busy airport lounge. His account was now the responsibility of a sister division, so we had not seen each other in several years. I could not help noticing that he was clearly uncomfortable, and having difficulty holding eye contact. After several minutes, I inquired, *"How are we doing with your account?"*

He proceeded to tell me that they had recently chosen a competitor's product for an important new business application they were about to introduce. *"I really like your company, you have been great partners. However, my business line manager could not get answers to his questions. He was uncertain that your product had the functions we apparently required. I didn't want to order him to select you, and I didn't have the time to investigate the specifics personally."* He proceeded to say, *"I even called the new division president to tell him that you were in jeopardy, but the questions never got resolved."*

Cannot give the final "Yes" but can sustain "No!"
that is why we call them Recommenders.

The Evaluators

We're going to get acquainted with two distinct types of Evaluators: the **Gatekeepers** and the **Coaches**. Each has a distinct set of needs and will require you to set Goals-take Actions-get Results. The challenge with all Evaluators is to understand their assignment and respond to them without losing sight of the end results. Evaluators have a primary investigative mission in the companies that employ them:

They are paid to get information, compile, sort, slice, dice and refine it, then to get more material, collateral, references or gossip about your product, your company and your competitors. Their goal is to make sure any decisions are analytic and factually correct.

The Gatekeepers

Early in my sales career, I did a major product presentation to a manufacturing firm in the Midwest. All the participants introduced themselves and their position in the company. As I customarily did in those days, I started the meeting by asking the audience to tell me what they needed to learn from my presentation. What knowledge was essential for them to hear about during our session? Within seconds, a very angry looking gentleman rose to his feet and announced loudly enough for most of Illinois to hear, *"Stop! No, you don't! We do not answer any more questions. You get to answer our questions! Then the meeting will be over!"* I had met the ultimate Gatekeeper. The good news (and the bad news) is that most Gatekeepers are more subtle and less verbal!

They care about, and you must focus on:
   1. Collecting information
   2. The evaluation process
   3. Control

This is not a particularly sales-friendly audience, and by its very nature, wants to control your access to other parts of the Selling Pyramid. So what are the goals we need to keep in mind when we work with Gatekeepers?

Just the Facts! Get the key details about your product/service documented. However, we do not want to be drawn into a "show me more" whirlpool by continually volunteering more and more material. Make sure your best features and functions stand out.

- Use your support team! Gatekeepers are not going to object to working with the real "product experts" in your company. In fact, they will thrive on the opportunity! Let the support team build this relationship.

- Work the Selling Pyramid! The Gatekeepers may object to this, but do not succumb to their desire to control your selling efforts. Use your selling team and executive management to open doors throughout the prospect account.

- Remember: People buy from people! The facts matter, details count, evaluations are important; but in the end, the Recommenders and Executive Buyers will make decisions based on need, value and judgment. Keep reminding yourself of this simple reality and act on it!

The worst selling mistakes take place when salespeople embrace

51

Gatekeepers, working hard to earn their affection and trust, hoping they will win the account with an approval from Mr./Ms. Gatekeeper.

The reason we often fall into this trap is that Gatekeepers always have time to learn more, and ask for more information. They are easy to access! We, by our very nature as salespeople, feel good about having found someone who is both accessible and interested in speaking with us.

The problem is they DO NOT make the decision to buy products and services. They cannot say "Yes" or "No" and sustain it. At best, they can recommend to a Recommender.

Ask yourself one additional question, *"What happens if I devote all my selling time and effort to Gatekeepers, and my competitor sells to the Cs, Executive Buyers and Recommenders?"* Enough said, we know the answer!

The Coaches

This is our second type of Evaluators. Coaches are those rare individuals with an interest in helping you and your company sell your product to their employer. Coaches can exist at any level in an account, but for now, we are going to focus our attention on the evaluator type of Coach. Who are these people and why do they want to help us succeed?

- They may have used our product in the past and enjoyed success.
- They may have worked with you, or your company, and are in a security zone.
- They may be personally comfortable with you.
- They may be misguided or misdirected.
- We may never know why or what need we fulfill for them.

While their needs are no different from the Gatekeeper, they are certainly more pleasant to work with. Therein lies the trap! We get lulled into our own desires for comfort, *"Sally really understands my product and its value. I can trust her to tell her boss and other decision makers about our solution. Everybody likes and respects her, we couldn't have a better advocate!"* I have heard and made those very statements. I have also lived to regret them! Work with your Coaches, seek out their advice; but judge for yourself whether their advice is good and should be acted upon. Manage your sales process and remember:

Never turn your account responsibility over to a Coach!
Coaches DO NOT buy product.

Right this moment, you may be thinking, "This is interesting, but, is there a way to know if I can really trust my Coach?" A couple of suggestions are in order:

- As you work all the points of The Selling Pyramid, pay a compliment about your Coach to another person. "I have really enjoyed working with Sally." Watch and listen for the reaction!

- Ask your Coach to deliver something substantial, "Can you get me a meeting with the Executive Buyer?" Observe the results.

Several years ago while immersed in a very competitive sales opportunity, I asked my Coach (whom I believed was an Evaluator despite his protests) to get me a series of meetings. Coach had assured me he could prevail with "our" solution because he was very experienced in getting things done at his company. I asked to meet the Executive Buyer. Unfortunately, Coach had never met that person, and seemed to lack a certain passion for trying. How about the CIO? Well, that did not seem to be achievable either. Eventually, I arranged a meeting with both the Executive Buyer and the CIO and called my Coach to let him know about the meetings. His response? *Wow, could you mention my name to the CIO? That would really be helpful to me.* I was glad to do that for him.

My advice with any and all Coaches is to verify before you trust!

The Targeted Selling Audience

A reminder that WHO you sell to will have a real impact on your success

Top Performers Sell To:

Primary:	Executive Buyers
Secondary:	Cs
	Recommenders

Average Performers Sell To:

Primary:	Recommenders
Secondary:	Evaluators
	Executive Buyers

Under Achievers Sell To:

Primary:	Evaluators
Secondary:	Recommenders

Final Reminders!

The Selling Pyramid is your roadmap to understanding the different organizational assignments of your prospects and customers. It guides you in responding to the needs that exist as a result of their assignments.

It gives you a clear picture of:

- Who you must focus your selling time on
- What the real needs of each audience are
- Why meeting those needs will enhance your sales results

Test Your Knowledge

The Selling Pyramid

1. The Selling Pyramid answers which two powerful questions?

    1._____

    2._____

2. List the five needs of "The Cs":

    _____   _____

    _____   _____

    _____

3. Executive Buyers personally make or control the   True/False
    final decisions on products or services because they
    own or control budgets and funding of proposed
    expenditures.

4. List the three needs of Recommenders:

    _____

    _____

    _____

5. Recommenders cannot give you a final "Yes" but they can
    say "_____" and sustain it!

6. Focus on Executive Buyers and ignore everybody else. True/False

7. The two types of Evaluators are : _____ and _____

8. Gatekeepers care about:
    A. Collecting information
    B. The evaluation process
    C. Control
    D. All of the above

9. Coaches are trustworthy friends to whom you can   True/False
    safely give account responsibility.

10. A Top Performer's primary selling audience is_____

The Business Sales Methodology

For Business-to-Business Selling

Roadmap Notes

To Salespeople

The ability to make a sale or even several sales does not assure you of continuous and predictable results. To achieve the long-term results allowing you to be recognized as a top performer in your vocation requires that you develop a methodology to manage your prospects and customers. That methodology must give you a systematic approach that can be measured, repeated and monitored as you lead your prospects to discover and act on the value you are offering to them. Our *Business Sales Methodology* gives you the foundation to create sustainable success.

To Managers

Leadership includes reaching your objectives in an organized coordinated team effort. Having a selling team composed of salespeople who go about their selling assignment in whatever way works for them places you at a disadvantage. The risks include delivering an inconsistent sales message, and not being able to control your sales strategy and tactical execution at a working level. Ask yourself this question: "Do I really know if each member of my sales team truly works from the same playbook?" Our *Business Sales Methodology* creates the commonality your team needs.

To Business Owners

The consistency of your "Top Line" growth and performance is very important to the success of your enterprise. Your sales team needs a predictable methodology to deliver new business from your current customers and prospects. A key element of the team's mission is to manage their accounts in a systematic, replicable and measurable process. Our *Business Sales Methodology* provides an efficient and highly productive foundation they can use to achieve your business sales projections.

The Business Sales Methodology

An externally focused selling process or methodology is the second integral continuum in *The Essence of Selling*. Adopting an externally focused sales methodology to manage your prospects is essential to sustainable success in the selling profession, and it's also a discipline many of us struggle to master and execute.

The problem with ignoring the need to have a sales methodology is that you end up dealing with each prospect in a one-off manner.

This leads to mistakes, oversights and a lot of time-consuming and costly experimentation. Much like building a house without an architectural plan, or driving in a foreign city without the benefit of a roadmap—it can—and is done. Unfortunately, the results are not always what we want them to be!

Prospects value and expect leadership from sales representatives! Exercising leadership is greatly enhanced by having a sales methodology to manage goals/ actions/ results and communications.

Some pundits will tell you, "Just focus on the customer...Let the customers decide on the selling agenda and environment that works best for them. Your job is to facilitate their needs and help them to establish value." This is supposed to result in customer-focused selling! Twenty-five years of selling has taught me that focusing on your prospect is fundamental. Unfortunately, many prospects either will not choose or will not self-manage the task of finding the needs your product meets or the value it provides. They expect and demand your leadership and competency in the evaluation process. They may choose to accept or ignore your efforts to lead, but they expect your full participation and attention.

Many prospects believe the quality of the sales performance they get before they buy is a key indicator of how well they will be treated after the sale is finalized.

As a vice president of sales, I would regularly call Executive Buyers and Recommenders at prospect accounts. One of the questions I would inevitably ask was, *"Has our salesperson met your expectations?"* The answer to this question fell into three general response patterns:

1. "Gordon is a real professional; he has been enormously helpful. His experience and guidance are obvious to our evaluation team."

2. "Gordon is doing okay; he does not seem to be very well organized, but he has worked very hard on our account."

3. "We have not been real comfortable or pleased with Gordon's selling efforts; he does not seem to have his act together."

The conclusion I reached as the result of these conversations is quite simple: Prospects want to work with salespeople who actively engage *The Essence of Selling* and who embrace the discipline of a sales methodology.

Why is it, then, that so many of today's sales experts never quite get around to the methodology issue? You will hear an occasional discussion or reference to "sales cycles," but the glamour seems to focus on the usual revelations about new tips and clever actions that increase your chances of immediate success by xxx percent. I think the answer is that in the hyper-expansionist environment of the late 1990s, the fundamentals of successful selling were relegated to an urge to find quick solutions to complex training issues. The ranks of new salespeople expanded rapidly and a premium was placed on getting sales results, rather than getting the fundamental skills right!

The reason a methodology matters is that, first, it's fundamental to sustaining successful selling. Prospects have an intuitive sense of ascertaining if you are working from a playbook or improvising. They also have a predisposition that tells them improvising may be acceptable, but it carries a risk. The risk is that your selling mistakes may hurt them if they choose to do business with you! Whether we are selling to small companies or global giants, the act of selling is itself a process with common elements, thereby allowing us to create an organized method every salesperson can easily use to get great results.

Second, methodology matters because "selling time" is the great equalizer. We are all limited by its finite nature. The more effort we, as salespeople, devote to creating a unique selling environment for each prospect, the more we reduce the efficient use of our selling time.

What do we want to accomplish with our methodology?

The Business Sales Methodology enables us to:
- **Lead our prospects step by step to the value they want and need.**
- **Monitor selling progress at the individual account level and for our entire portfolio.**
- **Engage in analytic reviews of where, when, and why we are encountering selling obstacles.**
- **Accelerate the closing of new business.**
- **Manage finite selling time.**
- **Repeat our success.**

To understand this better, let's define the common terms *sales cycle* and *sales process* and how they differ. Most experienced salespeople will attempt to discover the sequence, selection and evaluation criteria a prospect normally uses before committing to purchase. We are, in fact, attempting to understand the "life cycle" of a sale from the start to its finish. How do I find suspects? Who is qualified? How do I define qualified? What questions do they ask? What demonstrations will they request? Do they want references or presentations? When will they ask for these things, or should I suggest them? The totality of these activities is typically referred to as a *sales cycle*.

In many businesses, the steps and sequence of the sales cycle may be documented and very detailed; in others, they may be sketchy and informally understood. Learning about the sales cycle may take the form of asking colleagues to share their experience, consulting with sales management, or trial-and-error observations from your own experience working with prospects. We tend to focus much too quickly on how long a period of time the typical sales cycle takes to reach conclusion. The real world answer is often very vague. "Well, some accounts close in 30 days, others take 24 months." A sales cycle is historical; it will often represent a consensus of the reality of selling your product. Sales cycles frequently do not reflect a conscious executive decision of how we can best lead our prospects to closure.

What most companies call a *sales process* is much more internally and operationally oriented. It tends to report on prospect activities (pipelines), and anticipated dates when we expect to close accounts (forecasts). All organizations need to legitimately manage, monitor and analyze these administrative essentials to operating business plans. Do not confuse management's need to monitor sales activities, with your need for an external customer-focused sales methodology.

There is a generally unwritten but powerful sentiment in many selling teams that says, "You tolerate the process stuff, politely acknowledge (but generally ignore) any sales cycle documentation if it exists, and get on with selling." The reason for this is that many salespeople have not made the connection between today's hyper-competitive markets and the need for a fundamental selling methodology. A sales discipline increases our chances for success in highly competitive markets. A generation of salespeople is still trying to relive the capital-flush 90s that were abundant with funded projects and the capital to try anything and everything that promised productivity. It has become increasingly clear the selling environment has changed—the stage is set to begin the process of rediscovering the value of a managed selling discipline.

Two departing thoughts before we move on—when you have fewer prospects with a predisposed agenda to buy products or services, you need to manage and work each opportunity as if it is your only opportunity...and it may well be! Secondly, the prospects have figured out that in hyper-competitive markets they can, should and must demand more from the executives and salespeople who want their business. The stakes are higher and real selling skills matter again!

The Business Sales Methodology (BSM) is designed to teach the fundamental skills and disciplines that need to be accomplished for a successful sales campaign. It sets out clear GOALS-ACTIONS-RESULTS and gives you useful information to help you achieve your objectives, step by step. Our methodology integrates sales, marketing, sales support and executive management activities, with defined contributions and responsibilities. You can modify our methodology, if necessary, without destroying its integrity; but it's more likely you will conclude certain steps are of less importance in your particular environment, and you will spend less time focusing on them. Our methodology is not designed for the Business-to-Consumer environment—it's strictly Business-to-Business.

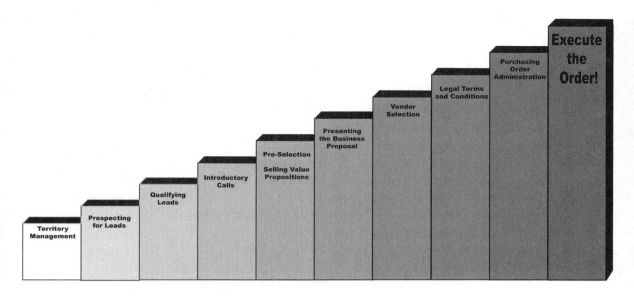

The Business Sales Methodology

Taking control of your selling assignment is the start of *The Business Sales Methodology.*

Territory Management

Goal: Identify the universe of potential accounts for which you are responsible.

Action: Access the knowledge bases that are available to you from public and proprietary data sources.

Result: You know what is in the territory.

Recently, someone asked my opinion about the worst way one can lose a sales opportunity. Is it: ignorance about your product's value? fail to understand your prospect's needs? or perhaps...being outsold by a competitor?

Several years into managing a geographic territory, I decided to attack a difficult prospect where our company had not succeeded in doing any business for many years. The buzz within our office was that we always lost at this account; the prevailing wisdom was that someone in power disliked our company. Undaunted by the facts, I managed to get an introduction to the CIO, who was surprisingly interested in hearing about our business. Sitting with this executive for the first time, I discovered he was a recent hire. As I started to review the products we currently offered, he had a look of pure astonishment and said, *"I am sorry I was not aware of your product; we just purchased a similar solution from the XYZ Corp last month."*

I had lost to an inferior competitor, without ever knowing about the opportunity. We always prevailed against them. That is the worst way to lose an opportunity—TO NOT KNOW—and not get the chance as a result of not knowing!

Territory management is about knowing.

Here are the five essential steps...
The first order of business in any sales assignment is to identify the accounts for which you are responsible. The accounts may already be documented, they may be a complete mystery, or a combination of both. You should start the identification process by accessing:
- Existing company or personal records
- External data resources
- Mailing list directories
- Commercial business directories
- Business database providers
- Industry reference lists
- Local business memberships in civic associations

The external resources can be obtained through free internet sites, but often you will have to purchase this valuable information. Make sure that whatever information you obtain is updated on a regular basis and comes from reputable sources. I always request a preview of the data, to be sure it contains the specific information I need.

Second, sketch out which companies are the "best fit" for your specific product:
- Target vertical market
- Asset size
- Number of employees
- Profile of existing customers

These sample characteristics, and others you will determine, allow you to sharpen your focus on your best "suspects." Why is this important? Remember our discussion about the finite nature of selling time? We want to be sure we focus our efforts on accounts that have the best fit for our solution. A business associate once told me "every" business was in need of his product. My response was "Great! But where have you sold it?" He proceeded to tell me that all of his best customers were independent sporting goods stores. My advice was, *"Concentrate your efforts on the hundreds of sporting good stores in our metropolitan area. Don't spend a lot of immediate selling time worrying about everybody else!"*

Third, create a database of key executives in each priority suspect you have identified. Who are the key players in the selling pyramid? Here is a sample of the information I would recommend accumulating:

Account Name:	Mailing Information:
Key Executives:	Titles:
Telephone:	Fax: E-Mail:

Most of this data is what you should be receiving from the internal information or external data sources mentioned earlier; some of it will be developed as you engage in the prospecting process. If you sell to publicly traded companies, an enormous amount of information is available about each of these businesses and it's accessible on the net.

Fourth, if you are fortunate enough to have existing customers for your product, put them to work for you! This, of course, assumes that they are happy customers! Introducing yourself to the client's key executives will pay enormous dividends.

Ask for two simple things:
- New business referrals.
- A good reference, when they are asked.

The reason most clients will go out of their way to assist you is that they understand a simple business tenet: success begets success. The more customers you have, the better their decision to do business with you looks, and the better the service they should receive. Finally, the information they share with you about your product will be incredibly valuable. Experienced salespeople have learned that the insight customers bring to you about your product reflects real world performance and value. What happens if I begin to manage my territory and find out an existing customer is dissatisfied? Personally, I would prefer to know sooner rather than later, and always take that dissatisfaction as a serious matter.

The actions you must take:
- Ask customers to reveal what they perceive to be the problem. Get them to put it in writing if possible.
- Make sure you understand their point of view and what they see as a resolution.
- Bring the issue forward to your management.
- Keep the issue on a positive path to resolution both within your company and with the customers.
- Finally, remember that quality companies take care of their customers because they understand it is both good business and the ethical thing to do.

65

What you must not do:
- Ignore the problem.
- Surrender your selling time to become an unauthorized customer service engineer.
- Blame your customer for the problem.

As difficult as this advice may be to accept, I would remind you that selling for a business that fails to make a commitment to customer satisfaction often becomes an unpleasant experience. Every business will have occasional problems satisfying customers; but when these become frequent or are viewed as acceptable, you have a serious issue that cannot be sold around.

For a short time, I worked at a company that had serious problems with its flagship product. The vice president of engineering proposed first to solve our problem by attacking the customers "who are not very bright." He then claimed that the problem was clearly a sales responsibility. My solution to this nonsense was to put him in front of the customer and let him explain his ingenious solution to the ultimate audience. As one of my customers said, "When I push the start button, nothing happens! How is that my problem or our salesperson's problem?" That company has long since been relegated to the dustbin of history.

We mentioned earlier the need to ask your existing customers to serve as references for your product, your company, and yourself. There are several important issues you should discuss and reach a clear understanding about with your reference accounts:
- The scope of the reference they will provide. Will they provide a detailed analysis of their experience or a generalized statement?
- Will they share any evaluations of competitive products they considered?
- Will they host visits by prospective buyers?
- Exactly who will provide the reference?
- Will they share "problems" or "concerns" they have about your product or company?
- How will references be scheduled? By whom? What restrictions on time or frequency will apply?
- What specifically will they say about your product and company?

The more complex and costly your product or service, the more important a customer reference will be. Do not assume that your reference will do or say what you define as the "right" thing! I have consistently found that unless you carefully choreograph and manage these events, you may find that your references can become the source of more confusion than enlightenment. Countless sales representatives play a version of Russian Roulette by just asking customers for references and then hoping for the best. They'll ask other salespeople to borrow their references and just assume good things will happen. Reference accounts are as valuable as you ultimately make them through good communication, planning, and execution. They deserve your close attention and constant nourishment.

A reference call that goes well is priceless; conversely, one that goes poorly can be a devastating blow to your selling efforts.

Fifth, find out which accounts in your territory are owned by your competitors. Instead of staying away from them as most of us do, make a special effort to introduce yourself and get acquainted. Why?

- You will learn invaluable information about your competition. You can learn their sales strategy, the product strengths their customers have identified, and what the customers believe they don't do well.
- You leave the door open to replacement business or other new business opportunities.
- It will make your competitors very nervous!

Listen carefully to the clients of your competitors; they are a very real source of information. Avoid the temptation to monopolize the conversation by attacking what you perceive as your competitors' failings. Listen and learn!

In one of my selling assignments, I called upon a prospect that owned several of my competitor's products. As part of my territory management, I was trying to sell them an unrelated solution that was completely divorced from the products they already owned. In the process of getting to know the key account executives, it became clear that they were very dissatisfied and just plain angry about the service they were receiving from our competitor. In fact, they volunteered and quite enjoyed taking telephone calls to tell how unhappy they were to anybody who would listen! In time, they became a customer, a great reference and one heck of a negative reference for my competition.

Territory management is extremely important and the starting point of our methodology! So, how do so many of us get off track and never get around to executing a true plan for territory management? For starters, we get impatient and chase the first opportunities to come along, which are typically inherited from our predecessors. In general, these inherited opportunities were left behind for a good reason—because they are flawed. In many cases, we waste precious selling time early in our assignment, only to realize suddenly that we are behind plan and in trouble.

As a Sales Manager, I always watched my new recruits closely to see what percentage of their early sales were inherited opportunities and which were truly of their own making. The fewer the newly created opportunities I observed, the greater the individual failure rate was destined to be. I cannot accurately recount for you how many salespeople, faced with an impending failure, would insist that they had "bad" territory, it was too new, or sold out, or whatever. They may have been correct, but the failure to create a well-executed Territory Management Plan made it impossible to tell if they were reflecting reality or not.

On my first day in sales, my predecessor stopped at my cubicle to tell me, *"You don't have a snowball's chance in hell of making quota in this territory. You may be smart and well liked but it's not going to matter. No one has, or ever will, make plan in this patch."* That very evening, I called a friend who had been in sales for a lifetime. He gave me a version of The Five Essential Steps to manage a territory. His product had no resemblance to what I was selling, the industry was completely different, yet none of those differences mattered. I spent the first four weeks each year identifying and calling every account in my territory; and as a result of that effort and discipline, I achieved at least 150 percent of my sales plan in each of the next three years! Territory Management is knowledge, and knowledge gives you the opportunity to succeed.

The very worst way to lose an opportunity is never to have known about it!

Prospecting for Leads

Goal: Open a dialogue with target opportunities in the territory.
Action: Hit the phones! Send the E-mails!
Result: "Suspects" for our product or service!

The second step in our *Business Sales Methodology* is prospecting. I like to refer to it as our lifeline to success, yet it's an act of heavy lifting. The simple truth is that very few salespeople like to prospect. In fact, most of us will go to great lengths to avoid it whenever possible.

68

Here are three caveats about prospecting:
- The more you prospect, the easier it becomes and the more effective you get.
- Top sales executives always have more than enough prospects; the mediocre do not have enough; and the failures do not have any.
- If you intend to be in sales for any length of time, you quickly realize that you may occasionally be fortunate enough to work at a company that provides you with qualified leads. However, sooner or later, you will be asked to stand on your own and prospect for leads.

Prospecting is a discipline!
It must be done continuously.
It must be done on a scheduled basis.

That's right, the key to successful prospecting is simple. Three words—discipline...continuous...scheduled! Prospecting is only a problem if you have forgotten about "Territory Management" and fail to execute on these three words of wisdom.

The metrics behind successful prospecting.
Every business day the number of suspects you uncover will have a direct impact on your sales results. Suppose your product produces one (1) sale from every 10 qualified prospects. To get a qualified prospect you need 10 suspects and, finally, 5 telephone calls are necessary to get one (1) single suspect. The metrics are simple (1x10x10x5): you must make 500 telephone calls to make a sale! If you only make 200 calls each month, you are going to really struggle to make your sale. Every business and product offering will have different metrics. The metrics can be affected by your marketplace, the competitive positioning or branding of your solution, demographics or a local economy, etc. Understanding the metrics behind making a sale will reveal the parameters you must use to guide your prospecting activity. Do some detective work and learn the metrics from the top sales performers, product managers, marketers at your business. Failing to manage this fundamental prospecting challenge can truly derail the achievement of your performance goals. Be prepared to adjust the methods you use and time you devote to prospecting, in order to get the metrics correct!

Whom do I call or e-mail to get the dialogue started?
Remember our discussion in *The Selling Pyramid*? The pyramid reminds us to focus on those who ultimately buy the products or services and the needs most important to them. There are two schools of thought about whom to call as we begin prospecting:

69

"The Contact-a-Recommender (or Evaluator) Approach"
This method is a bottom-up approach. Its proponents argue that it allows for easier access to organizational information, and scores high in the sales comfort zone. We may as well get to know the project managers and system analyst because we will have to work with them under any circumstance. Work your way up the selling pyramid.

"The Contact-an-Executive Buyer (or 'C') Approach"
This is top-down account penetration. Find out what needs executive managers have, then advance your solution to meet their business requirements. This is a tougher audience to get an opportunity to engage.

Never start your account penetration at the bottom of the selling pyramid; working your way up the pyramid is difficult and dangerous.

Returning from a long road trip, I received a terse message from the executive vice president of a key account. He demanded that I be in his office the next Wednesday at 10 a.m. I had never called upon or met Mr. Taylor. I knew his managers; they were my key account contacts. I was in the middle of a very difficult competitive sale there; and candidly, I had stepped on a few egos in making my argument for our solution. The meeting started tensely with a stern warning that I had annoyed and insulted several of his subordinates. Not good, but the root cause was that I had gone over and around several very territorial executives to make my case. Taylor asked me how I had managed to annoy his VP of IT so thoroughly.

"Look, this account is very important to me and my company. I've sold your company several highly successful solutions with great financial paybacks. The product I am proposing is brand new, very strategic, and a great financial fit for your needs. Yet, somehow I've gotten tangled in the wrath of the VP of IT."

Taylor looked at me and said, *"Okay, if this product is so strategic, why didn't you come to me and tell me about it? Why try to sell a strategic product to a manager with a tactical assignment? From now on, you come to me and tell me about any new solutions that reduce my operating expenses. I will decide if we're going to pursue them and who will work on the evaluation. Did you forget that your proposal eliminates IT jobs? They may not be exactly anxious to consider it!"* I had been introduced to top-down selling before it became a fashionable buzzword. I never went back to working my way up the selling pyramid again!

Prospecting scripts can be incredibly useful if you put them to work in the way we intend you to use them—as a starting point—for you to modify, based on your own success and failures as you prospect!

We have enclosed a sample set, but you can easily find countless other examples at bookstores, on the web, or from other professionals.

INTRODUCTORY VOICE MESSAGE

"The Script"

1. Name. Position and Company
2. 15-second statement about your company
3. We would like to tell you how we can help you:
   - Increase revenues
   - Reduce expenses
4. Issue a call to action:
   - A personal meeting, telephone call or web conference, etc.
5. A name and telephone number

The 24-hour Follow-up:
   - Ask for "The Chief's" Administrative Assistant.
   - Name and Company
   - "I left a message for 'The Chief' yesterday. I am concerned that I missed his/her call."
   - Ask for an appointment to speak with "The Chief."

ADMINISTRATIVE ASSISTANT CALL
"The Rules of Engagement"

Their responsibility is to be the designated blocker and keep unknown callers, such as sales representatives and a multitude of others, from potentially wasting "The Chief's" time. They are encouraged to take their assignment seriously. However, they also can become invaluable allies because they control executive access and calendars.

- Never get on their "wrong side" with argumentative or confrontational behavior. Polite and friendly is the rule of order.
- They are only a challenge when you are trying to make "First Contact."
- Keep in mind that once you are "certified" by "The Chief," they become a valuable resource.

"The Script"

1. Name, Position and Company.
   Is "The Chief" available?

   *I always use a Mr./Ms salutation, rather than Bob or Sally.

2. If the AA inquires as to the nature of your call:

"I would like to acquaint 'The Chief' with our Company and how we can assist him/her, just as we have helped the XXX Corp. and the YYY Corp. to grow their revenue and reduce expenses. This is an introductory call that should take no more than five minutes."

- Local, competitive or high-profile references will work best. Discussing your product with this audience is not advisable.

- Remember to relax your voice! If you sound nervous, flustered or uncomfortable, the AA will be reluctant to put your call through. He or she doesn't want to be embarrassed! Confident and personable resonates...practice!! By-pass them by: calling early, or late, in the business day or calling at the noon hour.

THE ADMINISTRATIVE ASSISTANT'S FOUR POSSIBLE RESPONSES

1st   The call will be put through.
See our Script for THE INTRODUCTORY CALL WITH THE CHIEF.

2nd   The Voice Mail option.
If the AA offers to put you through to Voice Mail, thank him/her and accept the offer. Review our INTRODUCTORY VOICE MESSAGE Script.

3rd   A request to send introductory material via E-mail or postal mail. "That's great, thank you so much for your help! I find that it's so much better for 'The Chief' to have the opportunity to review my material before we talk."

Ask for his/her name and quickly send the information with a short note attached. Announce that you will call him/her on a specific date to verify that the introductory material has arrived and to speak with "The Chief."

4th A refusal to assist.
This will not happen very often, but if it does, here are sample responses, all of which are delivered in a cordial tone and manner. The message is that we are too important to ignore and too persistent to be easily dismissed.

- "I can appreciate that you're very busy, but I am sure that 'The Chief' will want to know about our company...many of his peers and competitors already do business with us!"

- "Would it be better for 'The Chief' if I arranged for my company's (CEO, President or Vice President) to give him/her a call? Should I schedule a time for that?"

- "Could you share with me why you feel 'The Chief' is not interested? I would personally appreciate the insight. Is there another executive in the company I should talk to?"

INTRODUCTORY CALL TO "THE CHIEF"

"The Rules of Engagement"

- Knowledge is power. The more you know about your suspect's company and "The Chief," the better your chances for a successful call.
- Personal introductions or references will greatly enhance your opportunity to succeed.
- Do not turn the Introductory Call into a presentation of your product. Why?
  - It's premature; you are attempting only to pre-qualify the suspect at this stage.
  - If the product is rejected through misunderstanding or miscommunication at this stage, you are done!

- Two things matter to "The Chief"...will this product:
  - Increase my revenues
  - Reduce my expense structure
  (Get this part of your message down cold; articulate it and back it up with references!)

- "The Chief" will always do business with people he/she comes to believe can help him/her personally and add value to the business.
- First impressions count!

THE INTRODUCTORY CALL TO "THE CHIEF"

"The Script"

This is your first discussion; be polite but not overly solicitous. Think of "The Chief" as a peer you can help!

- Name, Position and Company
- 30-second statement about your company. Mention two reference accounts that are in the same industry or same geography, or being used by his competitors.
- A neutral Statement: "I am not sure we can assist you, but it would be very valuable to both our companies if, in fact, we can." (This will position you as a savvy businessperson.)
- A 30-second "Value statement" on how your product has helped other clients—grow revenues/reduce expenses.
- Ask for an appointment (personal meeting, telephone call or web conference) to jointly explore in greater detail how your solution may help "The Chief" grow revenues and/or reduce company expenses.

Review The Selling Pyramid for our advice about the "Needs" of each audience.

- If "The Chief" agrees to the appointment, express your thanks; confirm the time and date of the meeting.

- If you are going to have colleagues join you for the appointment, I suggest you reveal their name and position to "The Chief."

- If "The Chief" declines a meeting, ask permission to send him/her a package of material about your company and product. Tell him/her you will follow-up on a specific date to review any questions that may arise. Then, ask "The Chief" if you should speak with one of his/her peers about your solution. "Have I called the wrong executive in your company?"

- If "The Chief" refers you to a member of his/her staff, express appreciation for his/her assistance. "I know you will want me to keep you up-to-date on our discussions with your company, so I will call you occasionally to brief you about our progress."

Qualifying Leads

Goal: Determine which suspects are prepared to examine the value of your product.

Action: Listen-ask questions-learn-analyze.

Result: Achieve a mutual agreement that your product appears to satisfy a need the suspect has admitted to having.

How do we turn suspects into prospects or qualified leads?

Qualified leads must meet four criteria:
1. The suspect has expressed or asserted a need for your product. Better still, the suspect admits to a "pain" or "problem" that your product resolves.
2. The suspect has a specific time frame to address this need.
3. A budget and funding exist.
4. The suspect is willing to act.

The point I want you to understand is that "suspects" do not graduate to "qualified prospects" based on what we, as salespeople, decide is best for them. What matters is that the suspect decides he or she has a need we can fill with our solution.

Ever wonder why most sales forecasts are not accurate? Why we can't get certain "prospects" to move forward? The answer is really simple—they were not qualified and were never really prospects at all. We may have had a great rationale and all kinds of justification for why they needed our product. Product management, marketing and sales management may all be in agreement. However, until the Executive Buyer admits to a need and meets our four criteria, you have a suspect, plain and simple. There is nothing wrong with working and selling to "suspects;" it is an important part of the selling equation. The focal point of the efforts you expend with "suspects" should be to get them to state an admission of need.

Top performing sales professionals have learned that some suspects will never become prospects despite their best efforts. They continue to work with the account, but it takes a backseat to "qualified prospects" who are the real focus of their attention. The ability to discern the difference between suspects and prospects is a critical factor in success or failure as a salesperson. Why? The finite nature of selling time!

Top professionals have also learned when to "fire" or disengage from suspects, and move on to the next opportunity which, I can assure you, is never easy to do. Amateurs cling to suspects! Why? They do not embrace prospecting and tend to hold on to any suspect they can find.

Qualification is a continuous process!

Okay, qualification is difficult enough, but the reality is that change is ongoing. What was agreed to yesterday can change tomorrow. Priorities, budgets, and decision-makers are all temporary. You have to qualify and re-qualify your prospects on a continuous basis. When they fail to meet our four criteria, we have to wage a campaign to get the account back on track or assign it a lower priority. Unfortunately, that can happen at any point in our sales cycle, even up to the time we close and get paid for our solution.

A final thought is in order...review the steps 2, 3 and 4 referenced above. They are no less important than establishing a self-admitted "suspect" need. In fact, in an economic environment that is capital restricted, it is quite common for suspects to tell you that, "We really need your product. Unfortunately, I have no budget or funding and cannot tell you for sure when I will!" Our chapter explaining *The Selling Pyramid* contains some good advice on why you want to have this conversation with Executive Buyers rather than Evaluators. Suffice to say, a suspect does not become a prospect until criteria 2, 3 and 4 are met.

Our next step deals with introductory calls, which you make either in person, by telephone, or through web-based meetings on both prospect and suspect accounts.

Introductory Calls

Goal: Qualify or re-qualify and build momentum.
Action: Listen and learn! FOCUS-ON-THEM!
Result: A specific mutual agreement that the account is qualified and prepared to undertake an evaluation cycle

Introductory calls are a learning experience for both the salespeople and the accounts they are calling on. You are trying to qualify the account as a prospect. The suspect is starting to evaluate if you and your company are people with whom they could do business if a genuine need is established. The suspect may be also "just looking," gathering information to be used later in evaluating future products to offer their customers, sizing budgets, and getting familiar with potential productivity improvements. In many industries, executives rely on contacts with sales representatives to keep their knowledge current about important trends. The point is that you really cannot assume anything during an introductory call other than you have been given an opportunity to listen and learn.

Unfortunately, for many salespeople, the act of telling takes clear precedence over learning to listen. It is why so many introductory calls lead to inconclusive results. We have developed a catch phrase, **FOCUS-ON-THEM**, to remind you what really matters in making the introductory call.

FOCUS-ON-THEM

First impressions really do count.
Observe both the people and company environment.
Company goals are what?
Understand by listening intently!
So what do they really need?

Open-ended questions encourage discussion.
Neutral statements.

Tough qualifying questions must be asked.
High-level value propositions and references must be revealed.
Extract the commitments we want.
Measure the call results.

The discipline of FOCUS-ON-THEM allows us to avoid the Four Catastrophic Mistakes of Introductory Calls:

- A "core dump" of product features and functions annoys all but the most detail-oriented evaluators, who do not make the decision to purchase any product or services anyway! It also casts us as being rigid and one-dimensional.
- Failing to learn and understand what the suspect needs and wants—which means we don't know why or how our solution is valuable to the suspect.
- Having no real meeting plan—which translates to we are "just visiting." Unfortunately, busy executives do not have a lot of tolerance for this, and will be unlikely to permit you to come back for another "just visiting" exercise.
- Failing to make a good personal or business first impression—which positions us to be eliminated quickly by our competitors, who are viewed as more professional or better potential partners. Remember, in the end, people buiy from people!

Several years ago, the CEO of our company asked me to cover a meeting for him, which was booked for the next day. I phoned the sales executive who was to call on us to tell him our CEO was out of town, and had asked me to cover this introductory meeting. My schedule would be very tight so I could only agree to a 30-minute discussion...and to please call me back if he wanted to review the agenda. My guests arrived a full 15 minutes late, without calling to tell me about a delay.

The salesperson's first statement was to ask why our CEO was not present. His yet-to-be-introduced partner reinforced that they always meet the CEO when they engage a prospective client. Being polite, I suggested that we have a quick meeting to get acquainted and learn a little about our respective businesses. They began, "We own our market; we are so successful that we really choose who we do business with. Our competitors are non-existent; they're second rate firms."

One minute into our discussion, the first impression vote was in! I remember the rest of the meeting as a one-sided, rambling discussion about how they did this, that, and the other thing. They covered each of the four catastrophic mistakes in a truly outstanding manner.

When the suspect is fully qualified as a prospect, we are ready to proceed on a mutually agreed upon pre-selection sales process.

Pre-Selection Selling

Goal: Persuade the prospect organization your product best provides the value they need and want.
Action: Engage the Selling Pyramid.
Result: Earn the right to present your final business proposal.

Pre-Selection Selling is perhaps the ultimate challenge of the sales assignment. You work hard to find suspects, qualify them and bring the prospect relationship to this stage. Now you must manage a selling team, develop a value proposition, create a selling message, and provide formal presentations. Each of these tasks will be foreshadowed by competitors, and challenged by a myriad of objections and obstacles. Relationships across the selling pyramid will be called upon, as you gather information and adjust your sales tactics. This will all be done to accomplish one result—to present your final business proposal and become the selected vendor!

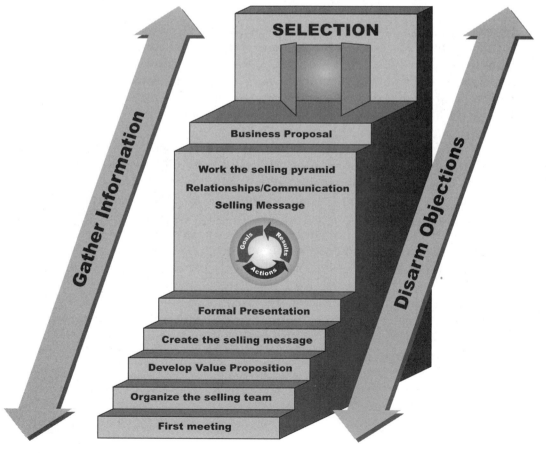

The First Meeting

The First Meeting is now behind you and covered in our discussion of Introductory Calls. FOCUS-ON-THEM still requires your attention. The challenge ahead can be best described with the word **VELOCITY.**

VELOCITY reveals how to achieve results in this stage of our methodology. Use it to remind yourself that:

Value proposition and a selling message matter.
Engage the full selling pyramid.
Lead your selling team.
Objection handling.
Close and qualify continuously.
I want your business!
Tell me how we're doing.
You sell the prospect what they need.

For most of us, selling is a team undertaking, especially if your product or service is complex and impacts different audiences in the prospect's account. Everyone in your company has to know his or her assignment in the selling process and what they are responsible for delivering. The salesperson must take charge of insuring that the selling team works together, presents a synchronized message and unified commitments.

A selling team that pulls together is a powerfully orchestrated force. When the opposite occurs, a lost opportunity is the usual outcome. It is easy at times to just assume that all those who are part of the sales process "will do their job."

Watch Top Sales Performers in action and you will see leaders who understand how to set strategy and then execute to the tactical details. Since their sale is on the line, there is little question of who is calling the plays.

In fact, those who work with these professionals will tell you they enjoy working in an environment where Setting Goals-Taking Actions-Getting Results is the order of the day. Less experienced or competent sales representatives often struggle to lead selling teams.

Committee Selling

B-2-B Selling is often performed in front of buyer committees. As if selling isn't challenging enough, it becomes more complicated when you sell to committees representing various buyer constituencies. The idea behind forming a committee to explore products and select vendors is that the buyer benefits from the collective strengths of a group composed of diverse talents and needs. The products they review and select receive broad affirmation and acceptance. The theory makes exquisite business sense. Unfortunately, committees present a challenge unto themselves.

Good team communication, effective management and positive dispute resolution are the hallmarks of successful taskforces—a combination of talent, skill and perseverance that's not easy to achieve. Salespeople must learn to work with well-run committees, as well as those that span the gamut of the good, bad and ugly.

Committee selling can be simplified by keeping the following disciplines in mind:

- First, learn the role of the committee. Will they have responsibility for selecting a vendor or will they be charged with evaluating and recommending? In particular, are they going to recommend one vendor or several for some executive's final consideration?
- What is the basis for their ultimate selection or recommendation? What are their needs?
- What time schedule are they working towards?
- Who's the executive sponsor? Who makes the final decision to purchase?
- Is this project or study budgeted and will it fund a purchase?

Qualify the committee as you would any other suspect! The qualification process should include discussions with the committee manager, senior participants and the executive sponsor. Listen, learn and ask open-ended questions. Occasionally, a committee manager will resist your qualification efforts, why? My experience has taught me that sometimes the committee head doesn't actually have answers to your qualification queries; on other occasions, he or she won't answer your questions because they know the end result of their activities will not meet your qualification test. "We just want to bring in several vendors to learn about the latest products, any decision to purchase is years in the future."

The scenario to avoid is investing time and resources presenting your product to a committee with an agenda you don't understand, or worse yet, is being withheld. Keep qualifying. Far too many committees end their evaluation efforts without any conclusive results.

Creating a committee with a number of important participants does not in itself mean a   purchase will occur. Spending your limited selling time with suspects who are not qualified or prepared to purchase is unproductive whether it's a single individual or a large impressive group. Which brings us to the ultimate committee question—Is the group representing a qualified prospect to purchase your product? Working The Selling Pyramid will help you answer this question.

The key to successful committee selling is to, first, view the task force as an audience with a set of needs you must satisfy. The committee may be acting in the role of an Evaluator, a Recommender, or rarely an Executive Buyer.

Secondly, continue to engage and sell to the individual committee members and every other target incumbent in the buyer's Selling Pyramid. The more effectively you penetrate the account, the more you'll learn the needs of individual Recommenders and the Executive Buyer. You'll build relationships and discover insights into the dynamics of the committee itself—knowledge that will help you set the goals, actions, and results necessary to win this business.

Don't fall into the trap of making the committee, and its project leader, the sole and exclusive focus of your sales campaign. It may take both courage and some strategy to avoid this mistake, especially when you have a project manager (Evaluator) warning you to restrict your sales activity to responding solely to his or her requests.

Organize the Selling Team

Sales assignments often require a group of talented professionals to work together to sell a product or service successfully. The more complex the solution you sell, the greater your reliance will be on other experts to help you achieve success. Learning to lead and manage an effective team is critical for many salespeople.

Teamwork starts with setting clear Goals-Actions-Results every member must work toward. Answer the following questions as you get your team organized and you dramatically increase your success quotient:

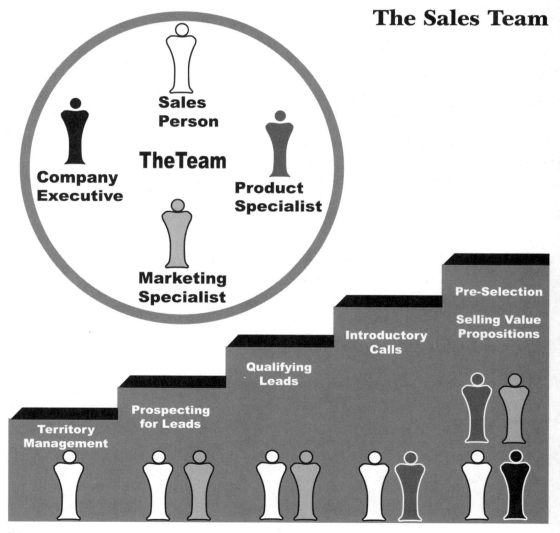

The Sales Team

- Who will ultimately be responsible for the selling team?
- Who will be part of the team?
- What will be the strategy for winning an account?
- What will be the primary and secondary contribution of each team member?
- As a group, when and how will team members communicate and coordinate activities with an account and how will everyone make the inevitable adjustments to the account sales plan?

A well-organized selling team is powerful!
A dysfunctional effort is a golden opportunity for your competitors.

Working Together

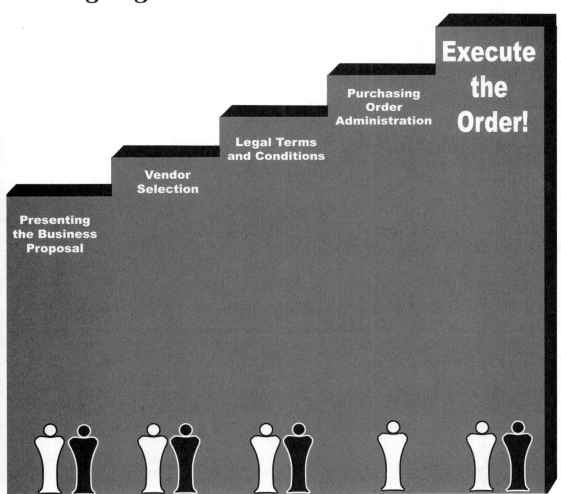

Experience has taught me that the biggest problem most selling teams have is the *"I assumed you would!"* challenge, followed closely by the *"Why did you do that?"* dilemma. The dynamic environment where most selling occurs is fertile ground for team communication issues. You minimize this challenge by having an organized plan to communicate and coordinate with each and every team member as you work through each step of the sales methodology. The team functions until the order is executed and value is delivered to the customer.

Who will be responsible for the selling team?
The simple answer is—the salesperson who owns the account. However, on occasion, an account will be so important to a business that a senior executive, or the owner of the company, will take personal responsibility for the opportunity. When this happens, it is imperative that this executive clearly defines what being "responsible" for the account really means. Will he or she take strategic responsibility, set the day-to-day sales tactics at each step of the process, neither, both or what? I have watched executives with good intentions and little sales experience lose key opportunities. Conversely, there have been brilliant performances by key executives who have stepped into the breach to assure important sales were won! Just be sure the ground rules for "extraordinary assistance" are clearly understood by every person on the selling team.

Who will be part of the team?
The team will typically include the following four participants:
- A salesperson
- A marketing specialist
- A product specialist
- A company executive

Team membership may be expanded if a unique expertise is required for selling your product—a very technical product may require engineering or scientific personnel.

When do they participate in the Business Sales Methodology?
What will be the primary assignment of each team member?

The Salesperson
He or she has ultimate account responsibility. He or she owns the execution of each step in the 'BSM' and has final accountability for the results of the sales effort. The salesperson has to lead the selling team and manage the coordination of assignments across *The Selling Pyramid*. Discovering the prospect's needs and leading him or her to choose the

value provided by your solution is the saleperson's decisive challenge and reward.

The Marketing Specialists
They provide a strategic portrait of why the prospect should choose to buy your product. Their early cycle work is instrumental in helping to identify the profiles of prospective accounts and helping to solidify qualification criteria. During pre-selection selling, they can add value by discussing the marketing plan for the product, review past and current success stories and reference accounts. Prospects want to have the comfort of knowing they are buying a well thought-out product that will have wide acceptance in their industry.

The Product Specialists
They are instrumental in the 'introductory call' and 'pre-selection' stages of this methodology. They have the difficult assignment of educating the prospect about the product, and are also responsible for verifying that the product will meet the expectations that have been communicated. The more complex your solution, the more essential this function becomes to the selling team's success. Evaluators on the prospect's team often view product specialists as impartial and valued participants. They should always maintain this unique position of respect and credibility.

The Company Executive
An invaluable resource to the selling team. He or she must convey two messages: first, the importance placed on this new opportunity, and second, a personal commitment to make every possible effort to ensure the prospect is well served by selecting the company and its proposed solution. Cultivating business and personal relationships with executives at the prospect's company is the added value this member of the selling team delivers.

Selling is often a team undertaking.
The better you are at managing a Selling Team,
the more successful you will become!

Develop the Value Proposition

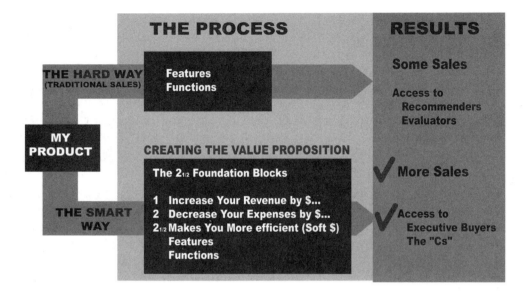

What is a "value proposition" and how do I develop it?

In the business world, this is a statement that tells your prospects that if they buy your product or service for x dollars they will earn profits of x+ dollars or more as a result. Our claim is supported by our solution's ability to increase the "revenue" or reduce the "expenses" of the prospect.

"Think about our proposal. Isn't it smart business to buy products or services that cost $1, and then allow you to earn many times that investment over the life of the solution?"

In today's business climate, this is the only type of product or services many companies will entertain and possibly purchase. In this example, the greater the cost multiplier your solution delivers, the more desirable it is! Sounds reasonable, right?

The challenge is that not every product or service can deliver "hard" evidence that it will increase the prospects' revenue and reduce expenses. In many cases, the profit multiplier exists but company executives, or we as salespeople, have not been able to articulate and quantify our value. Here is my best advice:

"Do It!" It is that important!

The two most effective ways to legitimize your value proposition are:
- **Use specific and quotable examples from reference accounts.**
- **Create a mutual proposition by asking your prospect if you can help them quantify the two 1/2 foundation blocks.**

Let's try a sample value proposition that we could imagine presenting to the Executive Buyer at a prospect account:

"Mr. Smith, I know from our last meeting that you are very focused on making your shipping operation much more efficient than it currently is. The current shipping process that you are using is, if I recall your exact words, 'inefficient, outdated, and far too expensive by industry standards. In addition, our customers are complaining about our levels of service. We are losing business!' (We have restated the prospect's admitted NEED/PAIN). Our sales team has worked closely with your management task force, and we have jointly concluded from our review that our BIG FIX IT product will meet your need for a highly efficient shipping dock. In the first 12 months, we have been able to identify labor and equipment cost savings that will pay for our complete solution. The increase in revenue BIG FIX IT creates will reduce the payback of your $5,000,000 investment to less than 6 months. We need to review the specific details..."

Create the Selling Message

Once you have developed a value proposition, you are ready to move on to creating a selling message. Executive Buyers are busy people. They are juggling lots of items in compressed time frames. We need to be able to deliver a short, concise message to them that clearly says, "This is why you should buy our solution!"

A quick story will demonstrate this concept for you, and it happens to be true. Traveling with salespeople is a large part of the job of any VP of Sales. After a meeting with several product evaluation engineers, the salesperson with whom I was traveling met by chance the senior vice president of the account we had just visited. We exchanged introductions and some pleasantries. Our salesperson then told the executive we had been visiting with several of his managers to discuss their project. The executive, glancing impatiently at his wristwatch, said, *"Interesting, I am waiting for a ride, but tell me again, quickly, why we should consider your solution?"* *"Well, you remember our product does this, does that, and also..."* the conversation was over before it began. Several days later, I watched a similar chance meeting play out in a different city, with a different prospect. This time, the saleswoman who owned the account responded as follows: "*Your people have told us the manual customer billing process you use is labor intensive and costs you millions of dollars in funds availability. Buy our product and we will cut your labor cost by 50 percent and allow you to recover millions of dollars in lost cash availability at your bank. You pay for your investment in 90 days, and get great service from our company along the way.*" Less than 30 seconds, but right to the point, and yes, we did get the sale.

The selling message—delivered in two minutes:
- **Restate the prospect's admitted NEED/PAIN.**
- **Summarize the value proposition.**
- **My company is a great partner.**
- **You can rely on my service and support.**

Formal Presentation

Does your product or service require you to do formal presentations? Before you voluntarily descend into "presentation hell," there are several rules and caveats I want you to remember! Presentations, done correctly, can help you win new business. Unfortunately, most presentations accomplish very little. Several studies have reported that the vast majority of attendees at presentations given by competing vendors cannot recall any distinguishing differences between the various presentations.

Here is my take on why many presentations accomplish so little:
1. Most presentations are in fact "show and tell" exercises.
2. They are often done before any prospect "needs" have been brought to the surface, explored or tested.
3. They are controlled by the prospect's Evaluators whose role is to gather and analyze information and quickly eliminate vendors.

During a regularly scheduled lunch with the CFO of a large account, I was asked by this executive, "*How did you guys ever lose the XXX deal to the Blah Corporation? Your service and support track record in our company and your installed products are far superior!*" I avoided responding with the real reason for our failure, but riding back to the airport, I recalled vividly how we had lost. Our account sales team, over the objection of their new sales manager, had agreed to "present" our product on very short notice and with no prior knowledge or attempt to understand the nature of our suspect's needs. The committee, a group of technical evaluators, eliminated us for lacking some obscure feature. When we objected to their decision we were told, *"Look, you had the same chance as 12 other vendors; you were eliminated. Stop complaining; it will hurt your future relationships in this company."*

The sales team, feeling threatened, acquiesced. A year later, when all the evaluators were either gone or long forgotten, the Executive Buyer was left to wonder what really happened and how he ended up with a poor solution. Having been that new sales manager, I knew we had entered "presentation hell," been trapped and lost for all the wrong reasons.

How do I get the most value out of the presentations I do?
1. Do your presentations as part of pre-selection selling. That means your prospects are qualified, you have jointly created a value proposition; and you have a selling message.
2. Insist the presentation be attended by Executive Buyers and the Recommenders, who will fund and use your product or service.
3. Do not make presentations for "suspects" and their evaluation teams. Instead, offer to do meetings or product reviews that allow for a joint exploration and discovery of needs. Work the selling pyramid to find the real buyers in the account.

The strategic message we want to convey at every formal presentation:
- We understand what you need from our mutual learning and relationships.
- Here is your value proposition.
- Deliver the selling message.
- Invite the prospect to access specific reference accounts.
- Quickly review key product benefits.
- Can we schedule a meeting to present our final business proposal?

Work the Selling Pyramid

The last topic we are going to touch upon in pre-selection selling is that of *objection handling*. Top performers will tell you that without objections you do not have a real prospect nor the opportunity for a sale. They are correct on both counts! This is also where your efforts at penetrating a prospect account across the full selling pyramid, and engaging in Setting Goals-Taking Actions-Getting Results, pays very big dividends. This is another way of saying that you should anticipate that objections will always be raised by multiple people at all levels of your prospect's account.

I like to sort objections into three broad categories:
- Business objections
- Feature/function/product objections raised by users of your solution
- Technical/engineering objections that may be more environmental in nature

Each of these challenges is potentially and equally threatening. I would suggest one final category: Are the objections an Annoyance or Deal Killer?

The first rule of disarming objections is to be sure they are all revealed. This approach is often referred to as "draining the swamp." It's a way of reminding us that solving half of your prospect's reservations still means that you lose! The same is true of Annoyances vs. Deal Killers. Fixing the annoyances is nice, but the deal killers have to come first, period! It is also a reminder to work the full selling pyramid. Resolving engineering objections, but ignoring deal killer business issues, will not get you what you want!

The second rule of objection handling is to keep asking a simple question: "If I solve these issues, will I be the selected vendor?" or "If I solve these issues, will I win your business?" Remember that it is more valuable to ask this question of an Executive Buyer rather than of Evaluators who may not speak with final authority.

In *The Essence of Selling*, we discussed communications as one of the base skills for successful selling. You may recall or want to reread our advice about listening and asking questions. Those skills are critical to resolving objections, and lie at the core of failed objection handling that happens when:
- We refuse to listen to the prospect's concerns or problems.
- We are so busy rebutting and arguing about each single objection as it is raised that we never encourage, allow, or insist that the prospect reveal all the objections.
- We convey an attitude to the prospect that is dismissive or condescending toward their questions about our product.

If your prospect does not believe you have a sincere interest in listening to and acting on his/her objections to your proposal, they will shut their communications down, and move on to the next competitor.

The third rule of objection handling is that honest effort counts.

The prospect wants to know that you and your company will diligently attempt to respond to their concerns. It is okay not to be able to fix each "annoyance" objection; most prospects do not really expect 100 percent resolution of their questions. It is also essential to simply tell the truth! "I cannot resolve this or that for you" or "Our product does not do that."

Objection handling also includes dealing with your competitors and their solutions. Remember that the competition will always be present because it is in the prospect's best interest to create a competitive sales environment. In general, prospects do not like negative selling. Your focus should be on the value you provide, not what someone else fails to do.

Sometimes you will be asked about a competitor or who your competitors are. You will occasionally be told that your competitor insists that your solution or company has certain failings or problems. The accusations may be accurate or outright distortions of the truth. In fact, the questions may be nothing more than a prospect testing you to see if the mention of a certain competitor strikes fear into your heart!

When you rebuff your competitors, the following rules apply:
- Do not engage in aggressive attacks that border on slander.
  Start instead with "XXX is a fine company but..."
  "Please do not take this the wrong way, I feel obligated to tell you...."
- Everything you say must be 100 percent factual and accurate. Never "go negative" with anything you are not 100 percent sure about!
- Your questions should focus on perceived big picture strengths, such as financials, references, or service and support, not some obscure product feature.

Prospects have a way of sensing fear—the more they believe you fear a competitor, the more nervous they will become. They also will feel slighted if you belittle a competitor; it insults the effort, investment and commitment they made in entertaining that proposal. If you have an issue your competitors always attack or you believe they will attack, reveal it before they do! This simple act will disarm the big news and increase your credibility. *"You are going to hear that we lost the XYZ account because of poor service. In fact, the truth is..."* (honest positive statement!)

I want to share with you comments I have had prospects reveal about objection-handling mistakes and how they reacted to them:

" We cannot get your competitor to tell us anything about their product. They are obsessed with telling us constantly how bad your product is. Our people are

93

tired of this behavior. We have decided to do business with you."

"The claims your competitor made about your product and company have turned out to be false. We know this because our staff discussed the information with your reference accounts and our own sources. I guess we cannot trust them!"

"They told us every customer they have is very pleased with their service and then refused to give us any references. At least your company had the integrity to admit to some problems and share your plan to fix them. We'll take our chances with your company!"

"They agreed to fix every objection we had, to anything we asked, even things we're not sure are really possible. Our engineers are now deeply suspicious that we are being misled, or that they are desperate for business at any cost."

Presenting The Business Proposal

Goal: Commitment from the Executive Buyer
Action: Meet with the Executive Buyer for your product or service
Result: Selection of the proposal

Let's quickly define the Executive Buyer, in case you have not read *The Selling Pyramid*. These are senior executives who control budgets and have the authority to fund those budgets. They carry titles such as executive vice president, senior VP or perhaps group vice president. They make the final decision on purchasing products or services. Organizationally they report directly to CEOs, COOs, and CFOs.

They care about four specific things, and you must clearly demonstrate your product and company can accomplish these for them!
   1. **Growing Revenues**
   2. **Reducing Expenses**
   3. **Increasing Productivity**
   4. **Enhancing their Career Aspirations and Image**

They matter because they personally have final responsibility for committing their organizations. I can assure you that they want to attach a name and face to any commitments.

The more strategic, unique or capital cost intensive your proposed solution is, the more critical your meeting with the Executive Buyer becomes. However, if your product is a commodity item or you are providing a reorder service for a product that is regularly consumed by your account in the normal course of business, you may choose to skip quickly through this discussion.

I strongly encourage salespeople, who are selling commodity solutions to make a point of engaging Executive Buyers at all their accounts. The meeting may be positioned as a simple courtesy call. Your efforts over time will pay great dividends in expanding your presence in the account, even if your primary buyer is a purchasing agent.

How do we secure a meeting with our Executive Buyer?

Since we have worked the selling pyramid correctly, we already know and have developed a relationship with the Executive Buyer. Remember this is exactly what distinguishes top performers from their peers! If you have not yet met the Executive Buyer, or if you have been blocked from him or her for a myriad of reasons, legitimate or not, you now have three fundamental options:

95

- Ask directly for the appointment yourself.
- Have a senior executive at your company ask directly for the meeting.
- Ask your senior contact at the account to facilitate a meeting—this is the most dangerous and weakest alternative!

When you get confirmation of the meeting, be sure to ask for any outstanding issues the prospect specifically needs to have addressed, arrange to have the business proposal delivered, and then test to close. *"We are looking forward to presenting our final business proposal and having you select us as your vendor."*

What's the purpose of the meeting? Why should the Executive Buyer agree to the meeting?

This is the culmination of the joint discovery process in which both companies have engaged. We are now prepared to share, summarize, discuss and defend why our solution best meets the prospect's needs! We naturally want our senior management team to personally make this commitment to the Executive Buyer. At this point, many of the attendees at our seminars will suddenly snap to attention and come to understand that having developed a relationship with the Executive Buyer and his or her staff early in the sales cycle makes this step very powerful and yet simple to execute. Conversely, the failure to engage this powerful part of the selling pyramid can now clearly put you at a true disadvantage to those competitors who really understand smart selling.

What is in the business proposal?

- A summary of the joint discovery process, highlighting the prospect's need and specific pain
- The value proposition
- The selling message
- Product benefits that matter to the Executive Buyer
- Financial terms and conditions
- Contractual documents

What can go wrong when I ask for the meeting? How do I respond?

- The Executive Buyer refuses the meeting.
  Action: Objection handling
- The Executive Buyer can temporarily defer the meeting.
  Action: Objection handling

In either case, you want to have a clear understanding of issues that are preventing your prospect from moving ahead and act to resolve them.

What can happen when we present the business proposal?
- The proposal is rejected.
- The prospect begins to negotiate parts of the proposal.
- The proposal is accepted and you are selected!

Rejection of the proposal requires you to engage in objection handling—remember to "drain the swamp," ask, listen, learn and then respond. The goal you wish to achieve is a full and complete understanding of the terms associated with the rejection and the reasons behind it.

Negotiation of the proposal is an intermediate step to closure. The vast majority of proposals will be subject to negotiation. The buyer may want specific concessions or need you to clarify specific parts of the proposal. Once again, you will be using your objection handling skills! The best sales are often the result of a meaningful give-and-take with the buyer—using your proposal as a starting point. The acceptance of your proposal is what you have worked for, now let's move on to the next step in the BSM.

Vendor Selection

Goal: Verify and complete the last agreed steps to final execution.
Action: Keep selling. Urgency matters!
Result: We engage the legal and/or purchasing functions.

The selected vendor, a blessing and a curse! Relax, the deal is yours! Savor the victory! Hey, nothing can go wrong, can it? What if...?

Being the selected vendor means that this opportunity is now clearly yours to lose. You can lose because you make an error or because circumstances undo you.

How can we make sure we do not proverbially, "snatch defeat from the jaws of victory?" Re-establish the prospect's internal process to finalize the order:
- Who, what, when, how and why needs to be involved with this order?
- What individuals, operating committees, and/or board committees need to give approval?
- What internal forms must be executed?
- Who is responsible for pulling the approvals together? Do they need help with presentations?
- Reach a mutual agreement on when each step is to be completed.

Push a sense of "urgent agenda" with your prospect.

- Every day we delay in finishing our transaction will result in the prospect losing revenue, while experiencing increased expenses and reduced profits.
- Get your installation and training commitments scheduled.

The pitfall we want to avoid is allowing your proposal to lose momentum. It is easy, and not uncommon, for prospects to move on to the next project, become entangled in the next crisis and never fully reach closure on our proposal.

Every day we linger as the selected vendor we are exposed to risks such as:
1. Buyer remorse
2. Competitors who focus on overturning your opportunity
3. Business disruptions at the prospect's company, including staff changes and financial setback
4. Business disruptions at your company
5. Broad economic or political events.

How many sales have been lost in the last two years as a result of budget freezes, key executives leaving or being reassigned, or mergers and acquisitions? The list of disrupting events is endless. In truth, many of these changes are beyond your control. The amount of selling time you have committed to get to this point in the selling process is significant and is not easily recovered. It is why "urgency" and "persistence" are so important at this and the subsequent stages of our *Business Sales Methodology.*

An old mentor always would remind me that, "As painful as it is, if you have to lose, it is preferable to lose early in the sales process. The worst losses are late in the sales process when your investments are more significant."

Legal Terms and Conditions

Goal: Finalize the contract.
Action: Get to the front of the line!
Result: Just internal paperwork remains

Not every product or service will require contracts or license agreements.

The use of a simple purchase order may suffice in many transactions. If your sale does not require you to interact with the legal process, congratulations! You can simply skip or skim through this step in our *Business Sales Methodology*.

The legal negotiation process is not designed to fail to reach agreement. Neither party considers that an acceptable result. The failures most often come as the result of the "time" exposure and changing business environments. The contract itself is designed to afford both parties sufficient rights, responsibilities and legal protections so they can prudently engage in a business transaction.

How do we get to the front of the line? Why does it matter? Top sales performers quickly learn several rules for managing the legal agreement procedure:

1. Learn your contract inside and out, its structure and the principles behind it.
2. Work in partnership with your legal counsel and the prospect's legal representatives; abdicating sales responsibility to participate in the negotiation process is a serious error.
3. Do not allow legal egos or personal agendas to prevail.
   The negotiations must go forward as quickly as possible. We want a deal that protects both parties in a fair and mutually acceptable manner. We do not want to wage a campaign that vanquishes one side or the other, driven by legal adversaries.
4. This is not the forum to restructure and renegotiate business terms and conditions that have already been agreed to. Clarifications are acceptable, but do not allow the legal staff on either side to hijack the sale.

What happens when, or if, we reach an impasse, and neither side will concede or compromise?

Philosophically, as salespeople, we never concede that an impasse has been reached! We may be in disagreement, but we are moving forward! The first order is to determine if a business issue or a legal principle is the sticking point. Business people—your executives and the prospect's executives—resolve business issues. Remind everyone that both parties have a significant investment in the proposed solution. Failure will reflect poorly on everybody involved in this negotiation. Keep negotiating! Keep escalating the issues to the Executive Buyer on both teams.

The Bottom Line:

- **Appeal to your Executive Buyers and selling pyramid allies to help expedite the legal process. They can move the agenda if they choose to intervene! Remind them that their financial justification is contingent upon getting the product delivered and placed into production.**

- **Negotiations should always include this statement: "Okay, we will concede on this point in return for your commitment to meet again tomorrow to finish the agreement!"**

- **Do not allow your company to be the cause of delay!**

Purchasing Order Administration

Goal: Get the paperwork finished.
Action: Leverage
Result: Final internal approval

Purchasing, as a function, can be an extraordinarily powerful decision center, or it can be a minor stop in the business of finishing an order. Unfortunately, the role of purchasing will vary from company to company. The nature of your product or service will often influence the involvement of the purchasing team. Office supplies are treated differently than million dollar equipment purchases.

The Role of Purchasing
- **Cost containment**
- **Continuity of business operations**
- **Process**
- **Vendor selection (variable role)**

"Get the best price and terms for the quality and quantity we need. Make sure we have the materials we need to operate, when and where we need them. Keep accurate internal records so we can authorize payment to our vendors in the agreed upon manner."

This charter does not include making life easy for salespeople or accommodating your interest in concluding this sale. The purchasing team, in fact, is compensated, evaluated, prepared, and trained to extract concessions from you. The assignment may or may not include deciding with whom the prospect does business and what products are selected.

Purchasing agents and their staff members who select products and choose vendors need to be treated as Evaluators, Recommenders or Executive Buyers. Question, qualify and re-qualify them to be sure they are the real deal and not pretenders. I recommend that you review *The Selling Pyramid* for sales strategies and tactics to effectively deal with each of these profiles.

How about the purchasing agents who just manage the order flow? How do I deal with them?

The Rules of Engagement
- Be polite, courteous and fair.
- Remember this is not a sales friendly audience.
- They get paid to squeeze vendors; they want price concessions, favorable payment terms, and special delivery schedules.

The Leverage Points
- Use the selling pyramid to push the need for urgency. The higher up the pyramid the better. *"I cannot ship without the paperwork!"*
- Do not engage in trying to "sell" or justify your product—that has already been accomplished.
- Do not get drawn into or provoke arguments or conflicts. We do not want to create excuses for a lack of cooperation that usually takes the form of delay in processing your order. These are usually busy people, who can easily find other vendor orders to concentrate on!
- Be prepared to offer concessions in return for "fast track" status—which means we consciously saved some negotiable items, because we understand the approval process.

Execute the Order!

Goal: Final order execution
Action: Set the date and time.
Result: Congratulations!

One of the many benefits of a sales methodology is that we have a step-by-step roadmap to follow. Many view final order execution, or closing, as a significant challenge. In reality, if you have followed our approach, it is a very simple task. Why?
- You know the prospect's purchasing/ approval plan.
- You know where you are with the necessary approvals.
- You know who owns the final execution step.

101

- You ask that individual two simple questions:
    1. *"When can I expect you to execute the order, so I can ship my product?"*
    2. *"How do you want to get the order to me?"*

So, why do so many salespeople struggle with closing?

Closing is a problem if you are groping in the dark, driven by fear, and uncertain of the prospect's agenda—hoping against hope to hear a "Yes!"

Twenty-five years in sales has given me a perspective on closing that is both comical and at the same time tragic. No salesperson enjoys being told, *"No, you cannot have the order"*—especially when the reason that "no" is voiced adds to the embarrassment and results in a loss of standing with the prospect. Here are some of the "no's" I have heard prospects express. Do any sound familiar?

- I can't sign this order, I just recommend to our committee. I am not even authorized to sign for $50.
- We have not yet selected the vendor we are going to consider; I don't know for sure if the selection will occur this quarter or next.
- We are not finished with our business case; until the project is approved, no orders are going to be signed.
- The committee actually selected your competitor several weeks ago.
- Sign the order?! We are still confused about what this product does for us.
- I wish I could, but we have a complex approval process I cannot override if I intend to stay employed.

The point of these real life examples is simple. "No's" are frequently the result of failing to exercise methodical sales leadership. We neglect to manage the prospect opportunity according to a distinct sales methodology. This directly increases the risk of not understanding at what step the prospect is in their evaluation, and who occupies the various roles in the selling pyramid. We end up trying to close with the wrong people at the wrong time!

The prospect is usually dismayed that we just did not understand their reality. We can recover from these errors, but not without damage to our credibility and relationships. Not many prospects will be comfortable selecting a solution championed by a salesperson that appears to have lost control of their account.

102

Does this mean that at this stage in our business sales methodology, nothing can go wrong? Unfortunately, even at this late stage, opportunities are occasionally lost or placed in peril. The roadblocks at this stage are represented by three major events:

1. A financial obstacle
2. A change in executive management
3. An environmental change in the business climate

I advise salespeople to start with one of two statements when confronting a late-stage roadblock:

"We have both invested heavily in making this partnership work."
"We clearly agree that you need the value our product provides your business."

These messages set the stage for a joint exercise in creativity, the ability to solve problems, to adjust and morph. The roadblocks may be temporary in nature or more permanent than we would like. The creativity exercise is designed to make the best of the problem at hand and keep the delay of closure to a minimum.

Some of your opportunities will fail to close at the very last step in our methodology, despite excellent selling work. Professionals learn to expect it, but work to minimize it!

Two Additional Steps after the Order...

Product Delivery and Customer Installation

Goal: The product is put to work.
Action: Manage the delivery/installation
Result: Value is realized and payments rendered!

Every person in sales either has learned, or will learn, from experience this simple reality: **The sale is not done until customer value is realized and the payments are received.** Your product may be simple and easily put to use, or it may be complex and require long installation or customization cycles. Your commission plan may be tied to delivery, production or payment events. Regardless, the reality remains the same.

Let's review several issues that are occasionally overlooked:
1. Customers need to be successful with your solution.
   - It's ethical business behavior.
   - They will provide references.

- Your existing customers are an outstanding source of new business opportunities.

2. Customers rule...Three simple actions that will eliminate 90 percent of your customer complaints:
- *"I will continue our communications and relationship."*
- *"I am fully committed to your success with my product, both professionally and personally."*
- *"Any questions, problems or concerns? I am available!"*

3. Honor the commitments you have made. Even when things go wrong? Suppose some of the problems are beyond my control? You should assume that, despite everyone's best plans and intentions, inevitably something will go wrong. When we start with that mindset, we are then prepared to act quickly and decisively when we are challenged. Whatever issues arise, one constant should remain, you honor the commitments you have made.

4. Keep an open mind and open dialogue about any representations you do not recall making. In general, these issues fall into three categories:
- Misunderstandings with your customer—*"I thought you said...I thought you meant...."*
- Customer oversights and mistakes— *"I forgot to tell you I really need this."*
- Customers will occasionally make errors and feel threatened by their mistake, or become fearful of the consequences. Some will attempt to place blame for the problem upon the salesperson, rather than take responsibility for the mistake.

5. You have to be prepared to "make it right" through compromise or renegotiations which impact the obstacles to their successful use of the product.

Does that mean we do anything a customer requests? No, it does not. It does mean we act in good faith and focus on doing what is right, not what is expedient or what we can get away with.

The most difficult decisions come when we realize we cannot meet our customer's expectations despite our best efforts, for reasons that are within the customer's control. When confronted with this reality, smart business executives will follow their organization's philosophical approach to dealing with dissatisfied customers. How does your business reconcile this challenge?

Up-Selling To the Next Opportunity

Goal: Today's customers = tomorrow's sale
Action: Keep selling to your customers
Result: More sales revenue and greater productivity

The first sale is always the most difficult. Why? As salespeople we face lots of unknowns, such as learning the selling pyramid incumbents. Executing to *The Business Sales Methodology,* we also begin to understand how our prospect makes decisions about needs, does financial planning and justifications. We explore how the legal and purchasing functions work. Across the company we build relationships and communication channels. All this information, or at least a significant portion, is reusable. You will hear yourself saying, "Next time I will do this or that, and not make this mistake again." Knowledge is power and it equates to productivity—an opportunity to work smarter and faster!

The first sale is also more challenging for the customer. They are evaluating a new company and its sales and service teams. They are also absorbing the risk that their new vendor will perform as promised. Ever wonder why experienced salespeople know that dislodging established vendors is hard to do? Here are some of the efficiencies that customers achieve by purchasing a second or third time from the same company, assuming that the first experience met, or exceeded, their expectations:

- Known entities reduced risk of failure or surprise.
- The efficiency of managing fewer vendors impacts profits.
- They benefit from greater vendor leverage in price, delivery, and service.
- Integrated product line opportunities may exist.
- Personal relationships and influence increase.

Each party to our new sales relationship has a vested interest in seeing that the first sale is just the first of many.

What prevents every customer from fitting in the exclusive group of clients we often refer to as *"the 20 percent who generate 80 percent of our sales?"* There are structural barriers, which primarily include offering only a single product that does not require reorders or expansion.

Sometimes our product lines do not meet any other customer needs. As salespeople, we have limited control of these obstacles. There are, however, self-imposed barriers that are by far the most annoying and most manageable:

- We failed in our initial sale to meet our customer's expectations.
- We simply forgot to ask, or we postponed asking for additional business!

Let's concentrate our efforts on this point.

The best time to sell more products and services is when the account is in the act of purchasing!

Remember, it is in the customer's interest to expand their relationship with you. Even if the request is premature, the act of asking sends a clear signal that you want the opportunity to meet their needs again; that will be viewed as positive under any circumstances.

Whom do we ask for more business? I always recommend starting with the Executive Buyers. They care about broad business needs, they own budgets and funding; and finally, they are the ultimate selling targets. Recommenders and Evaluators may have an interest in additional product opportunity, but only if the products fall under their span of control.

Final Reminders!

The Business Sales Methodology allows us to:

- Lead our prospects step by step to the value they want and need.
- Monitor progress at the individual account level for our entire portfolio.
- Engage in analytic reviews of where, when, and why we are encountering selling obstacles.
- Accelerate the closing of new business.
- Manage finite selling time.
- Last, but not least, it may be used repeatedly for continuing success!

Wisdom may dictate that adopting a sales methodology will increase your chances for success. I can assure you that using our *Business Sales Methodology* will position you for certain and demonstrative selling success!

Test Your Knowledge

The Business Sales Methodology

1. The problem with ignoring the need to have a sales   True/False
methodology is that you end up dealing with each
prospect in a one-off manner.

2. List four benefits of The Business Sales Methodology:

      _____

      _____

      _____

      _____

3. What is the basic concept and importance behind a Value
Proposition?

      _____

      _____

      _____

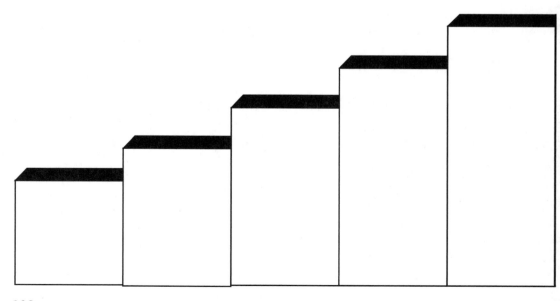

4. The first rule of disarming objections is to be sure they are all revealed, better known as "_____."

5. Aggressive attacks on your competitor that include   True/False
slander and half-truths always work!

6. Always present your Business Proposal to what incumbent on the Selling Pyramid? _____

7. Fill in the 10 steps of The Business Sales Methodology on the chart below:

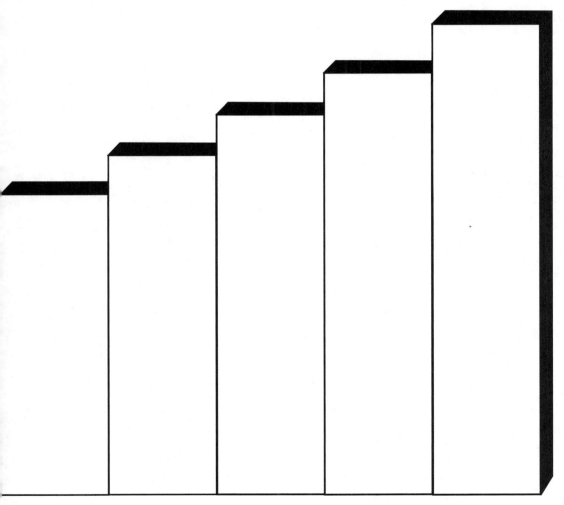

Forecasting Your Sales Results

Roadmap Notes

To Salespeople

Creating accurate forecasts will accelerate your success. Your finite selling time can now be focused on accounts that are ready for closure, and you will gain a clear view of your future business opportunities.

To Managers

Most selling teams struggle with forecasting. Unfortunately, missing a forecast, or not having the "runway" to allow you enough time to deal with inaccurate sales projections, is one of the critical factors that influence your ability to be successful in your assignment. You have to develop a sales plan, act to close business, and you have to do it on schedule. This chapter will help you create an environment to do just that.

To Business Owners

The challenges of running your business, making smart decisions, and creating a solid plan for the future, are directly tied to the visibility of your sales results. A difficult economic environment makes the need for accurate sales projections even more critical. *Forecasting* provides you with foundational, thought-provoking ideas and concrete tools that will allow your team to improve the accuracy and reliability of your sales projections.

The Forecast

A forecast is a window into our future performance as salespeople, set against a specific period of time. We have a view of which sales opportunities we believe are ready to move to closure and when that will happen. Or do we? Suppose our forecast is wrong? What happens then?

The larger the business, the more complex the sales forecasting process becomes. However, whether your business is large or small, one fact remains constant: An accurate forecast is critical to manage a business effectively; an inaccurate projection of your sales performance can be devastating to an organization and to everyone who is part of the enterprise.

The business press is replete with stories about financial executives at public companies complaining that they have little confidence in the forecasts they are receiving from their sales teams. Without this information, even basic financial projections are of questionable value. Sometimes, you will hear that the projected sales have been lost; on other occasions, the problem is that the opportunities have been delayed. These deferred sales may not be lost completely, but may have slipped into some future month, quarter or year. The problem is not unique to public enterprises; it impacts millions of private companies all across the business spectrum.

Let's look for a moment at some of the key business challenges forecasting impacts:
- Support for new customers
- Inventory and raw material requirements
- Staffing requirements to manufacture, deliver and support the product
- Facility planning
- Cash flow requirements
- Profits
- Planning for the future direction of the enterprise

I'm sure you could add other issues to this list! Misjudging any one of these subjects can severely damage a business; collectively, they are lethal. Companies of all sizes and financial resources have failed because they misunderstood their sales opportunities.

Despite all the discussions and hand-wringing about the need for accurate

113

forecasts, in my opinion, the intellect, discipline, and methodology to improve how well we individually and collectively forecast continues to languish. That does not mean forecasting is easy to improve or that there is a magic algorithm that can be applied to make this challenge disappear, but....

Let me sum it up with a piece of common wisdom:

You can make it happen!
You can watch it happen!
or
You can continue to wonder what the hell happened!

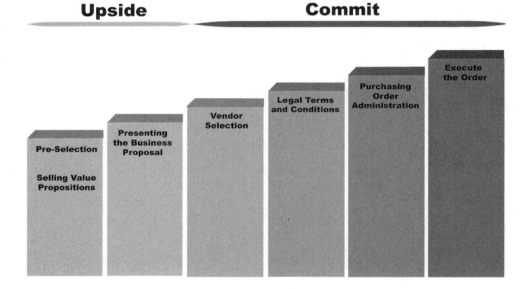

How can you create accurate forecasts?

All forecasting starts with individual salespeople and rolls up through whatever organizational hierarchy you have collectively embraced. Forecasting is not a top-down exercise.

The first order is to focus on the importance of creating accurate forecasting. Executive management and the VP of sales have to promote the important role forecasting plays in the operation of the company. Individual sales representatives have to embrace its value on a personal and business level, and commit to working toward the accurate disclosure a successful business requires. Every business–no matter how small or how modest the expectations–needs to forecast sales results.

Second, you need a culture that promotes and rewards accurate disclosure. The trap often faced in achieving accurate disclosure is both complex and adversarial. It works like this:

- When your sales team achieves plan, there is often little emphasis or interest in exploring how plan was reached! You justifiably celebrate the accomplishment and move on. What people fail to examine is, *"Did we close the opportunities we projected? If not, why not? Were there surprise closes, and why did we miss them in our original projection?"*

- When results disappoint, group and individual interrogations begin! *"How could this happen, who is to blame for this? This better not happen again!"* If this sounds all too familiar, it's because it takes place in businesses on a regular basis, big and small, simple and sophisticated.

- The signal sent to the sales staff from these actions suggests that the smart approach to forecasting is to promise nothing—that way if they do deliver a sale, they will be praised. Perhaps, more importantly, they will not be criticized for failing to deliver anything because they made no commitments. Salespeople who continue to produce wildly optimistic forecasts that never materialize are removed or disciplined, which sends a further reinforcing message. Sales representatives who either refuse or are permitted to make no committed forecast are eventually removed, but they survive for longer periods of time.

- Companies often lack a common sales methodology and common terminology to evaluate a prospect's status. Sales reps add to the challenge of the forecast process by stumbling over verbiage. *"Oh, you thought I meant this account would really close this month! Actually, I didn't promise anything other than my best effort to close it. Unfortunately, the budget is still up in the air!"*

- The sales management team is then forced to perform "surgery on uncooperative patients" in order to extract something approaching acceptable sales projections. Executive management has little confidence in sales forecasts that have shown little or no accurate results, and should not be asked to rely on them!

- The financial people begin to factor the projections up or down. In the end, no one is really accountable for anything concrete. The sales management team quickly realizes they are in a lose-lose environment. Executive management distrusts the forecast, and the salespeople resent being forced to make commitments.

You can create a culture that supports accurate forecasting:
- Value and compensate salespeople for selling the product and services their sales plan requires.
- Value and compensate salespeople for achieving the forecasts they commit to deliver.

Reward sales representatives who understand that forecasting is simple and valuable. The reward system can include more lucrative commission arrangements, bonus payments or countless other forms of recognition. Anyone who has managed a team of salespeople, small or large, quickly comes to understand that most sales behavior can be focused with a written sales plan that sets clear and demonstrable rewards for the performance you desire. Accurate forecasting is no more nor less achievable than any other sales challenge, if managers make it a point of focus and reinforce it through a compensation plan! In fact, we have enclosed a sample Sales Compensation Plan.

Promise what you can deliver...and deliver what you promise!

Third, salespeople need to embrace the fact that accurate sales forecasts are important to their personal success. Sales representatives often ask me why they should care about forecasts? *"What's in it for me? I don't want to be held accountable for this task! Why go through all the trouble of getting it right?"* I believe there is a simple answer! It will make you money, each week, each month and every quarter.

Forecasting is a basic part of your sales assignment. It deserves your best professional efforts.
In my selling career, it took me several years to understand how to break the cycles of "feast or famine." There is a tendency for most salespeople to get several well-qualified prospects and work those opportunities to closure. They focus all their energy and effort on those key opportunities and convince themselves this is the correct action to take. When sales are finalized, they victoriously come up for air only to realize that the pipelines are essentially empty! Now, they are months away from the next real sale. It is a disheartening cycle and essentially means they are starting

116

the selling assignment all over! It is also a point at which many sales people decide to find another job rather than restart the process. In time, you learn the value of continuous prospecting and working a sales methodology and forecast system that clearly gives you a view of what you have to do to create a predictable revenue stream. This reinforcement reminds you to take the tactical and strategic actions necessary to replenish your pipeline before it runs dry and panic sets in.

Compensating for accurate forecasting adds increased focus to the process. Remember, our goal is accuracy. The rewards are forfeited if you miss the forecast by either exceeding your projection or by failing to reach the projection. As an example, the starting point of this policy may be to say that all salespeople must submit their forecast within x days or weeks of the reporting period. The forecast must be accurate to the 90th percentile for qualification to receive the program bonus. Sales representatives should be expected to explain and defend their forecast as part of this process.

Top sales performers understand that forecasting is essential to the business they work at or own. Salespeople who view the task of forecasting as creating unnecessary, or unappreciated stress, need to be reminded that selling is ultimately about delivering results on a projected timetable, for all the reasons discussed earlier. It is very easy to lose sight of the impact a forecast has as it rolls up through an organization.

The best of intentions aside, misleading yourself and others with a misguided sales forecast serves no purpose. This leads us directly to our next challenge.

Fourth, you need a business sales methodology to create the foundation for a forecast that is accurate. If you do not have a customer-focused methodology for managing your prospects to closure, you have no consistent basis for deciding who is going to close and when. The alternative is your *best intuition* which is not exactly the ideal foundation for successful selling. The sales management team is also exposed trying to consolidate commitments that come from salespeople with disparate definitions of when a particular opportunity will close. I have attended sales meetings where some sales representatives will forecast the imminent closure of opportunities they have yet to qualify, or meet, based on an intuition. Other salespeople at the same meeting will only forecast business that is in the process of "cutting purchase orders." Getting everyone to work from the same playbook, with a common foundation and terminology, can quickly solve this very common problem.

The Business Sales Methodology

This would be an excellent time to review *The Business Sales Methodology*. Our methodology takes you step by step through a business sale with the necessary *Goals-Actions-Results* at each stage.

You build your forecast from the sales methodology and integrate your forecast with the methodology.

Let's do a quick review of what we want our methodology to accomplish for us:
- Monitor progress at the individual account level for our entire portfolio
- Allow us to engage in analytic reviews of where, when, and why we are encountering selling obstacles
- Lead our prospects step by step to the value they want and need
- Accelerate the closing of new business
- Use repeatedly for continuing success.

After merging the results from each individual sales representative and selling assignment, you begin to create a consolidated organizational picture. You know how many accounts are in "pre-selection selling" across your organizational units, how many "selected vendors" commitments exist, etc. Sales management and executive management can then begin to observe, apply, analyze, and manage the metrics you determine are essential to successfully manage your business.

The Business Sales Methodology becomes the forecast template. The first point of focus is on pre-selection selling. To reach this point, you have qualified your account and performed "introductory calls."

Remember, to "qualify" means to achieve a mutual agreement that our product or service appears to satisfy a need the suspect has admitted to having.

The suspect meets our four criteria:
- The suspect expressed a need for your product or admitted to a "pain" or "problem" your solution resolves.
- The suspect has a specific time frame to address this need.
- A budget and funding exist.
- The suspect is willing to act.

During "Introductory Calls" you execute to the following:

Goal: Qualify or re-qualify and build momentum

Action: Listen and Learn! Focus-On-Them

Result: A specific mutual agreement that the account is qualified and prepared to undertake an evaluation cycle

(All of this material is covered in detail in *The Business Sales Methodology.*)

When you enter into "Pre-Selection Selling" you work to the following agenda:

Goal: Persuade the prospect organization your product best provides the value they need and want

Action Engage the Selling Pyramid

Result: Earn the right to present your final business proposal

A closer look at the activities included in pre-selection

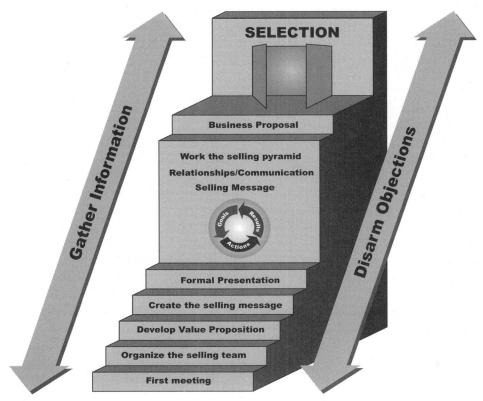

The Four Simple Rules
for Accurate Forecasting

RULE #1

Forecasts are done on fixed schedules with a standardized format. Everybody with sales responsibility produces a forecast, undertaking the forecasting exercise multiple times during a financial reporting period.

Deciding how frequently a forecast is prepared will be based on the nature of your business. For example, if you sell expensive products or services with long selling cycles, you may want to forecast on a monthly schedule. Products that have shorter sales cycles and are volume oriented may be projected on a weekly basis or several times each week. You will also be guided by your need to do financial reporting. Public companies are focused on quarterly and annual reporting periods. Many privately owned enterprises do financial reporting monthly, quarterly, and annually. Forecasts should provide guidance for and coincide with your accounting periods.

I have provided a template of a sales forecast you can tailor to your specific needs. It is essential that your forecasts are all done in a standard template so there is no confusion about the individual and group disclosures that are taking place. Nothing is more frustrating than sorting through disparate forms, all of which provide similar but different information while the success of your business hangs in the balance. This is also the same underlying reason that no one with responsibility for sales revenue is exempted from submitting a forecast. You cannot project what you do not know about! What you do not know can and will hurt your business.

Since you will be doing standardized forecasts on a scheduled basis, you will have advanced indications of how your company will perform before the end of any financial reporting period—information that allows you and your business to adjust, respond and manage the impact of positive or negative sales trends. As you progress through your financial reporting period, the forecast should begin to tighten and provide greater clarity of

120

projected performance.

The accounts you are projecting and tracking will have progressed through our *Business Sales Methodology* or will be stalled for various reasons. You will have a more finite sense of how much has to happen for a prospect to become a customer in the forecast time you have remaining.

RULE #2

Accounts that have not entered into pre-selection selling are not eligible to be placed on a forecast!

Evaluate all accounts in the status of pre-selection selling as potential "upsides." These are opportunities that can potentially be brought to closure in a defined forecast period but would be a stretch to finalize. The time period is of your choosing: it can be a week, month, quarter or year. The important point is that these accounts, promising but incomplete from a selling prospective, are where you concentrate efforts to cover the potential shortfalls you may discover in your sales projections.

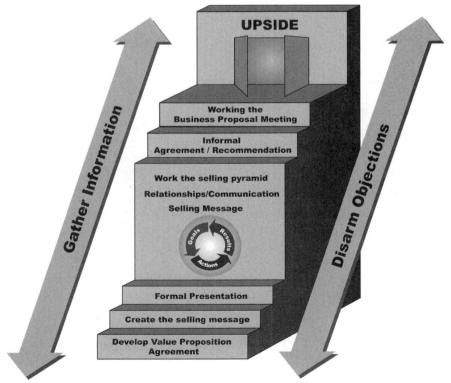

To forecast an account as an "upside" you must:
- Be clearly in pre-selection selling.
- Have reached a mutual agreement on the acceptance of the value proposition.
- Be informally selected by a Recommender in the account.
- Have ongoing dialogue with the Executive Buyer.
- Be progressing to the business proposal meeting.

RULE #3

Your goal is to have enough "commit" accounts to meet or exceed the sales projection toward which you are working. Your experience will guide you to the "overage" in commits you will need to safely achieve plan.

To regard an account as "commit," you must:
- Have been formally notified that you are the selected vendor.
- Have an agreement to execute the order by a specific date, which is within the forecast timeline.
- Have a mutual plan with your prospect to monitor the execution of the order.

RULE #4

"Upside" accounts are fallbacks that are available for replacing "commits" that fail to close on schedule, and become future "commits" as you move forward.

I never recommend counting on "upsides" to cover more than 20 percent of your plan. You should target having three dollars of "upside" prospects to cover each dollar of "commits" that you may be lacking. You can refine these metrics as you gain forecast experience with your specific environment. I frequently hear, "Isn't forecasting supposed to be much more complicated?" The truth is that many organizations have made

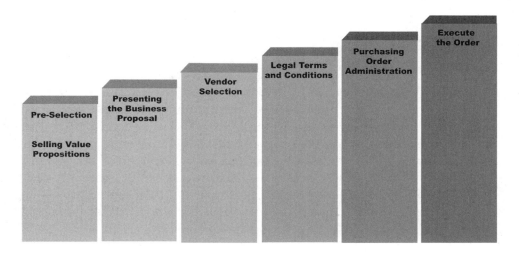

forecasting more complicated than it has to be. At times, companies overreact to a vexing problem by developing complicated account-rating systems, set against a equally complex percentage-to-close factoring formula. A friend observed not long ago, *"How do I forecast 75 percent of a deal? —especially if I only have one opportunity to close! If the opportunity is for $100,000, I am going to deliver either zero or $100,000. I will not deliver $75,000 on the forecast!"*

My advice is, keep the forecasting process simple and get your organization behind it. Once it is up and working well, then begin to refine it; and that may include making it more complicated. Just remember, your goal is accuracy. I believe that complexity is only valuable if it refines accuracy.

A quick review of the components of effective forecasting:

1. The forecasting discipline must become a point of organizational focus and be part of the sales compensation plan.

2. Forecasts are done on fixed schedules with standardized formats. Everyone with sales responsibility participates.

3. *The Business Sales Methodology* becomes the forecast template.

4. The criteria a prospect must meet to be ultimately forecasted as an "upside" or "commit" are clearly defined.

Value of Accounts

How do I determine the monetary value of the accounts that are forecasted?

It is not uncommon for a forecast to be accurate in predicting which prospects will come to closure in a given timeframe, but to completely misjudge the dollar value of the final sale amount. Welcome to one of the complications of getting an accurate forecast! Salespeople are often challenged by prospects trying to decide not just to purchase the product, but having a multitude of decisions about optional features that may be provided, and ultimately the initial quantity they will order. Everyone wants to sell prospects the maximum amount of product they can be persuaded to order. Here are my suggestions for forecasting when you face this challenge:

- Forecast the minimum order size as a "commit" and "upside" any additional revenue.

- Avoid the temptation to forecast the largest or most optimistic order configuration without fully disclosing the "risk" involved in the transaction. I have seen incredibly optimistic account forecasting turn what was a great order and sales victory into a psychological disappointment due to unrealistic expectations. I have also seen sales lost because sales representatives pushed for order quantities that were unrealistic because of forecasting blunders.

- Discuss your "dilemma" with your prospect and ask for advice. I can assure you it will precipitate a very valuable and mutually informative discussion.

Should the sales forecasting process be automated?

The simple answer to this question is Yes! The complex part of the equation becomes how to apply the many possible forms of technology that are at your disposal in a way that gives you real value. I like to look at technology in this instance as a way to:

1. Accelerate the collection of forecast data.
2. Sort, analyze and track both current and historical forecast data.
3. Quickly distribute the forecast throughout the entire enterprise.

The type or degree of technology you apply should not burden your business by creating more work than value. You may decide that a simple spreadsheet application is sufficient, or that this task requires a sophisticated salesforce automation solution. I have listened to numerous sales representatives and managers express frustration with salesforce automation projects that have become data entry nightmares, and in the end, deliver marginal results that are occasionally referenced by sales, sales management or other company executives. Technology should not be viewed as a way to take business judgment out of forecasting or to replace that organizational responsibility. Instead, it should be seen as a tool, or set of tools, that is flexible enough to make your forecasting methodology efficient, accurate and accessible.

What is the difference between a forecast and a pipeline?

It is easy to confuse these two terms. A **forecast** is composed of upsides and commits, both of which have minimally entered into at least pre-selection in our methodology. A **pipeline** is your forecast, plus accounts that are qualified but not yet in pre-selection. In our methodology these accounts are reflected in the "qualification" and "introductory call" stages. I often refer to these accounts as qualified suspects. Pipelines are useful for watching and analyzing early-stage sales cycle activity.

A note of caution about pipeline activity is in order. Early-stage sales cycle activity is very speculative and can be misleading. Qualifying an account is not a one-time exercise. You constantly re-qualify as you progress through a sales cycle. The simple fact is that early in a sales process you will initially qualify a suspect for your product. That may well qualify the new prospect to be placed in your sales pipeline. Unfortunately, many of these prospects will fall by the wayside as you enter into "introductory calls" and "pre-selection selling."

The real value of pipelines, at an individual and company-wide level, will come from comparing the value of your current data to historical data, and extrapolating trends. Large and robust pipelines should not be viewed as a substitute for closed business, a reason to relax, or an excuse to kick back.

A mentor once observed that individuals and enterprises that were struggling always had large pipelines. He would refer to this phenomenon as the curse of an optimistic sales mind speaking to management's happy ears.

125

The Pipeline Template

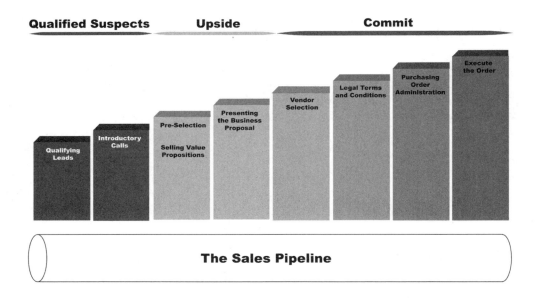

Qualified Suspects — **Upside** — **Commit**

- Qualifying Leads
- Introductory Calls
- Pre-Selection
- Selling Value Propositions
- Presenting the Business Proposal
- Vendor Selection
- Legal Terms and Conditions
- Purchasing Order Administration
- Execute the Order

The Sales Pipeline

Should I track prospects that have dropped off a forecast?

The answer is Yes! We have provided you with a Lost Prospect Analysis to help you do just that. The value of this exercise is to allow you to analyze both the "upsides" and "commits" that failed to come to closure. At the levels of both an individual sales representative and a company, this information can give you a picture of why business is being lost and how to correct the problem. I encourage you to call the Executive Buyers, Recommenders, and Evaluators at each prospect to get their individual perspective. My own experience is that you will be amazed how freely most people will speak and share information with you. Losing an order is always painful...losing late in the cycle is both painful and expensive!

Here are just some of the difficult issues you should be probing:
- Who was awarded the business? A competitor, or was the purchase cancelled? Perhaps the prospect solved their need with an alternative solution that your company did not offer?
- Did your sales team meet the prospect's expectations?
- Was your selling message or value proposition clear, and did the prospect understand the value of your offering?

126

- Are competitors exploiting a real or a perceived weakness in your company, products or service?
- Are you truly qualifying the prospects? Or are you now discovering that you were working with prospects that had never really been qualified?
- What does the prospect perceive to be the strength and weakness of your product and the competition's solution? Ask the same question about the companies themselves.

You may want to assign someone in your company other than the salesperson of record to ask these questions. The final piece of wisdom I will leave you is:

"To have a meaningful discussion, you must listen, be sincere in soliciting the prospect's input, and avoid defensive comments or judgmental behavior." If you cannot behave like a "good loser," as difficult as it may prove to be, then the value of this exercise will be greatly diminished. Unfortunately, you then lose twice!

Questions frequently asked about forecasting

I have only one or two deals I work on at any one time; is forecasting really necessary?

I believe that when you work with a small number of prospects you have to be extraordinarily focused on winning each deal. Forecasting becomes an important tool in helping you understand all the details of your opportunity. Secondly, forecasting also reminds you that having more than one opportunity is really paramount to increasing your chances for personal success. I am always mystified about the one deal at a time question. What you need to ask is, *"Am I working one deal at a time because I choose to do this, or is the market for my product imposing this reality on me?"* My experience is that this is often a self-imposed issue!

I have lots of small deals for which I'm responsible; forecasting seems like too much effort to me!

I would argue that the way to get the most efficient use of your selling time is to get organized, especially in the environment where you are working. Forecasting will give you a clear roadmap of which accounts need your immediate attention, when they need it, and then allow you to manage them to closure. You also get the benefit of being able to project your results into the future.

Can I have more "commits" than I need to make my plan? Should I forecast being over plan?

You certainly can have more "commits" than you need to make plan; it is a great problem to have. Just remember that not all your "commits" will necessarily come to closure and some percentage of your "upsides" may close. I would not hesitate to forecast being over plan; just remember to use your best judgment, and make the forecast as accurate as you can. In a moment of euphoria, do not make the mistake of setting expectations you cannot deliver.

Should I ever forecast missing plan?

This is always a difficult position to be in. The answer is simple: disclose reality. The only thing worse than missing plan is misleading yourself and others by forecasting things that are not going to happen. Use this setback to develop a plan to move your prospects to closure for the next reporting period.

It appears to me that whenever I do a forecast, the inquisition from my manager begins! Am I missing something?

Twenty-five plus years of sales experience has taught me that one person's idea of an inquisition may be another's image of a fireside chat. That aside, there are several reasons that you should be doing a forecast, even if it's only for your own benefit. First, you will get a clear picture of how your current sales efforts are paying off, and what *Goals-Actions-Results* need to come next as you manage your key prospects to closure. Sales professionals realize their businesses need forecasts to survive and prosper. They understand that creating accurate forecasts is a win-win. I will also wager you that the more accurate your forecasts become, the less unpleasant the inquisitions will become.

What do I do with sales representatives who just refuse to cooperate in doing a forecast or who claim the exercise costs them valuable selling time!

This is a common challenge sales management faces. It is also why I suggest tying forecasting to sales compensation plans. If you take this action, a failure to forecast or do it accurately will cost your salespeople money. That is not something they will ignore. At a deeper level you will need to reinforce that forecasting is important to your business and their ability to achieve personal success. In my experience, most salespeople who ignore forecasting do it because you allow it to happen, or they fear being held accountable. Both situations need to be addressed whatever the circumstances.

Our collective "commits" and "upsides" really do not come close to my business plan. Where does that leave my company?

One of the values of a forecast is that it prepares you for reality and gives you an opportunity to make adjustments. You can either take extraordinary actions to move prospects through the steps in our sales methodology or you can disclose, rethink and revise both your sales and business plans.

We do not seem to have an organized system of forecasting, yet we spend enormous amounts of time in meetings about making plan. Any suggestions?
Start your next meeting by spending an hour as a group reviewing this chapter. I suspect you can quickly agree to implement our forecasting methodology.

Final Reminders!

Forecasting has three constituencies: Business Owners, Managers and Salespeople. Executives need the fundamental business knowledge that comes from accurate and timely forecasts. Managers need a clear target list of prospects for closure, time to act to persuade those prospects, and a picture of individual sales performance. Salespeople need forecasts as a self-generated report card of their work efforts and a path to financial success.

Forecasting is difficult and, in many cases, painful, because it forces one to face reality, pleasant or not, and then to act on that reality. The difficulty applies in equal measure to business owners, managers, and sales representatives. Forecasting emphasizes that a disorganized selling effort reverberates throughout the business and has a far-reaching impact.

Our approach to forecasting can and will improve the accuracy of your sales projections. The approach is systematic, and provides common terms and foundations everyone can use. It is integrated with a concrete sales methodology. It will not burden your organization with meaningless complexity. The incentives for rewarding accurate disclosure can quickly be incorporated in your sales commission or compensation plans. Accurate forecasting is driven from the bottom up in an organization. The templates provided here allow you to forecast, consolidate and examine lost opportunities at an individual and enterprise-wide level.

A commitment to accurate forecasting is the first step you need to undertake. The guidelines presented here will help make that step a simple but powerful statement for you and your organization.

129

Forecasting
Your Sales Results

WORKBOOK

Forms and Templates

Workbook Instructions:

Sales Forecast Forms
We have provided you with three levels of Forecast forms, each designed to roll up to the next reporting level.

    1. An Individual Prospect Forecast
    2. A Sales Representative Forecast
    3. A Consolidated Forecast

Pipeline Forms
We have provided for two levels of Pipeline disclosure information.

    1. Sales Representative Pipeline
    2. Consolidated Pipeline

Lost Prospect Analysis
We encourage you to use this form and its questions to start your examination of lost sales opportunities. You may want to modify and customize the questions as you gain experience with the discovery process.

Sales Compensation Plan
This sample plan is provided to remind you of the necessity of having written sales plans. It also integrates the sample rewards for accurate and timely forecasting.

Upside/Commit Definitions
A handy reference guide of the requirements for forecasting an Upside or Commit account

Notice: The forms included with this publication are proprietary and have been provided for the exclusive use of Lawrence Group LLC customers and their employees. The forms may not be resold or distributed without our expressed written consent.

Prospect Forecast

| Date: | Sales Rep: | Business Unit: | Forecasting Period: |

Prospect Name:

Product:

Name:

Key Prospect Contact(s):
- CEO/CFO
- Executive Buyer
- CIO
- Recommender
- Evaluator

THE "Cs" — CEO · CFO

EXECUTIVE BUYERS — EVP · SVP · Group VP
Business Executives with Budget

THE CIO
Technologist Who Recommends

THE RECOMMENDERS
Vice Presidents of Directors
Department · Product · Functional Managers

THE EVALUATORS
Consultants · Project Managers · Technical Specialists
Coaches   Gatekeepers

Upside   Commit

Pre-Selection
Selling Value Propositions

Presenting the Business Proposal

Vendor Selection

Legal Terms and Conditions

Purchasing Order Administration

Execute the Order

Current Status

Current Account Status:
- Upside
- Commit

Value of Sale:

Next Step

Next step in Methodology:

Date to be accomplished: ___/___/___   Estimated date of final execution: ___/___/___

Assistance Required:

133

Sales Representative Forecast

©2004 The Lawrence Group LLC

Date:	Sales Rep:	Business Unit:	Forecasting Period:

Upside

Commit

Pre-Selection	Presenting the Business Proposal	Vendor Selection	Legal Terms and Conditions	Purchasing Order Administration	Execute the Order

Selling Value Propositions

Forecast per prospect

Amount per category

Prospects

Forecasts per category

Total Forecast

Consolidated Forecast

Date:	Sales Rep:	Business Unit:	Forecasting Period:

Upside

Commit

Pre-Selection

Selling Value Propositions

Presenting the Business Proposal

Vendor Selection

Legal Terms and Conditions

Purchasing Order Administration

Execute the Order

Forecasts per sales rep

Amount per category

Sales Representatives

Forecasts per category

Consolidated Forecast

135

Sales Representative Pipeline

©2004 The Lawrence Group LLC

Date: .... | Sales Rep: .... | Business Unit: .... | Forecasting Period: ....

Qualified Suspects   **Upside**   **Commit**

- Qualifying Leads
- Introductory Calls
- Pre-Selection
- Selling Value Propositions
- Presenting the Business Proposal
- Vendor Selection
- Legal Terms and Conditions
- Purchasing Order Administration
- Execute the Order

Forecasts per prospect

Amount per category

Prospects

Forecasts per category

Total Sales Rep Pipeline ....

Consolidated Pipeline

©2004 The Lawrence Group LLC

Date:	Business Unit:	Forecasting Period:

Qualified Suspects   **Upside**   **Commit**

- Qualifying Leads
- Introductory Calls
- Pre-Selection
- Selling Value Propositions
- Presenting the Business Proposal
- Vendor Selection
- Legal Terms and Conditions
- Purchasing Order Administration
- Execute the Order

Sales Representatives

Amount per category

Forecasts per category

Forecasts per Representative

Total Consolidated Pipeline

Lost Prospect Analysis

©2004 The Lawrence Group LLC

Date:	Prospect Name:	Sales Rep:	Interviewed by:

Prospect

Title: _____

Contact info: _____

Position in Selling Pyramid:

- ☐ CEO/CFO
- ☐ Executive Buyer
- ☐ CIO
- ☐ Recommender
- ☐ Evaluator

Why were we eliminated:

- ☐ Planned Purchase was canceled
  - Why? _____
- ☐ Elected to solve the "need" in a different way.
  - How? _____
- ☐ Selected a competitor. Who? _____

The Interview

Questions; did we....   Answers   Rating

1 2 3 4 5

Sales Team
- Listen to your Business Challenges?
- Understand your need?
- Present our solution?
- Explain our Value Proposition?
- Other?

Product Solution
- Explain our F/F/B?
- Meet your requirements?
- Perform Demonstrations?
- Present References?
- Other?

Company
- Explain our Business Mission?
- Introduce our Executive Management?
- Discuss our Cust. Support and Service ?
- Other?

Share with us what you perceive as the strengths/weaknesses of our competitor and ourselves:

_____ (continue on backside)

138

Sales Compensation Plan
XYZ Company

Date:

Calendar Period of This Plan:

Sales Representative:

Sales Assignment/Territory:

Authorized Products/Service to be sold:

Quota Assigned: $000,000. per annum

Target Annual Income:

Base Salary:

Commission and Bonus Plan:
- 2% on the amount of all sales up to your assigned quota.
- 3% on the amount of all sales after you have exceeded your annual plan.
- $1,000 p.a. bonus for timely submission of all required monthly forecasts. All forecasts are due the last business day of each month. Bonus is payable quarterly.
- $1,000 p.a. bonus for accurate forecasting. The achievement of 90% of your forecasted sales performance is required. The VP Sales may approve the payment of this bonus, if you exceed both your forecast and plan.

Sales Plan Terms and Conditions:
- How and when you get paid commission....
- How your employment status can affect commission payments...
- We reserve the right to make the following revisions....

Legal Obligations and Disclosures:
- This plan is/is not a binding contractual agreement....
- Disputes are resolved by.....

Company

Sales Representative

Upside/Commit Definitions

Upside Accounts Must:

1. Be clearly in pre-selection selling
2. Have reached a mutual agreement on the acceptance of the value proposition
3. Be informally selected by a "recommender" in the account
4. Have an ongoing dialogue with the "executive buyer"
5. Be progressing to the business proposal meeting

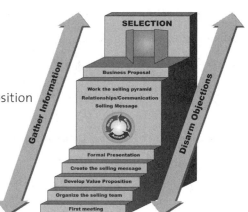

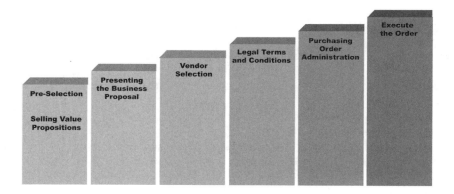

Commit Accounts Must:

1. Have been formally notified that we are the selected vendor
2. Have an agreement to execute the order by a specific date, which is within our forecast timeline
3. Have a mutual plan with our prospect to monitor the execution of the order

Test Your Knowledge

Forecasting Your Sales Results

1. An accurate forecast is critical to effectively manage   True/False
   a business.

2. Salespeople need to embrace the fact that accurate   True/False
   sales forecasts are important to their personal success.

3. Define both the terms "Upside" and "Commit"

   _____

   _____

   _____

4. What is the difference between a Pipeline and a Forecast?

   _____

   _____

   _____

5. Building your forecast from a sales methodology will   True/False
   cause confusion that you can easily avoid.

6. List The Four Simple Rules for Accurate Forecasting:

   1._____

   2._____

   3._____

   4._____

7. Name several important reasons to track "lost prospects" from
   your pipeline?_____

   _____

   _____

8. What are some negative ramifications a business will face with
   an inaccurate forecast? _____

   _____

The Ten Personal Skills of Top Sales Performers

Roadmap Notes

To Salespeople

Success in a sales assignment and a career is often determined by your commitment to excel. We help you answer the question, *"What kind of salesperson am I today?"* We'll show you the personal attributes and skills to reach the top levels of performance.

To Managers

Your responsibility is to recruit, train, and lead the best-selling team you can assemble. Getting the best performance from your team starts with helping them reach their full potential. The difference between mediocre and exceptional sales results often comes down to individual personal performance qualities, which you can influence! Assisting each of your salespeople to grow beyond their current capabilities will pay enormous dividends.

To Business Owners

Your business is best served by having the most professional sales team that you can recruit, develop and retain. What actions can you take to significantly improve the personal performance of each sales team member? What would be the impact at your company if each of your salespeople produced 20 percent or 30 percent more top line sales? This chapter is designed to help you make this opportunity a reality.

The Ten Personal Skills

Once you have obtained a sales assignment, and the challenges of being new to this profession begin to lift, you will ask several important questions. It will not matter if you actively pursued the opportunity to be in sales or were dragged kicking and screaming into the role of selling product or services. Ultimately, you will ask yourself: *"Do I enjoy being in sales? Is this something that fits my career plan? Does working as a salesperson meet my current and future personal financial goals? Is this what I really want to do?"*

If the conclusion you reach is positive, you have taken a major step toward success! The very next question you will ask yourself is quite simple! *"How do I become a Top Performer?"*

If you are driven and committed to be in sales, then you will want to be a top performer!

You will quickly come to understand that the rewards of being a top performer are significant at many levels. Financial security, performance awards, peer recognition, and ongoing accolades are just a few of the benefits bestowed on those who succeed in sales. Perhaps most important is the realization that you are making a difference to the customers you serve and to your company. Top salespeople are clearly very valuable assets to every business. Their care and feeding becomes very important to the organizations they choose. The path to management responsibility, or the ownership of a successful business, often starts with becoming a top sales performer.

145

Conversely, the agony of being a mediocre, or even worse, a failing salesperson is never ending. In my 25+ years of selling, it was always very clear that there were the top performers, those who were on the way to becoming top performers, and finally, everybody else. These "on the bubble" salespeople live in constant turmoil and often suffer the effects of stress. Some of this pressure is externally imposed but much is often self-imposed. Being confronted with the uncertainty of not knowing if you belong or will be accepted in a sales organization can be traumatic. These salespeople struggle to survive in a competitive profession that values and rewards results—yielding little or no job security nor other rewards for salespeople who do not perform.

Just reflect on the fact that in almost every business, large or small, employees throughout the company know which salespeople are bringing home new orders, and supporting everyone's job security. They also know that salespeople who fail to deliver expected results are jeopardizing the company's well-being. Talk about peer pressure and being on the spot! Those who have experienced this scrutiny will tell you it can be very unpleasant.

Once you have committed to being in sales, you realize that reaching the top of your profession is both within your grasp and a necessity to achieve. You will observe many of the top performers in your business and peer groups and conclude that it is possible for you to achieve the same success they are enjoying. The simple fact is, if you want to succeed in sales and you are willing to work at learning how to be successful, you can and will reach your objective!

This chapter is going to teach *The Ten Personal Skills* that will make you a Top Performer. Our focus will be about motivation, mindset, and action. The best news is that each of these qualities can be learned, practiced, and improved. You just have to commit to being open to learning and acting to reinforce your personal proficiency!

1	**High Energy**
2	**Focus**
3	**Fearless**
4	**Urgency and Persistence**
5	**Positive Attitudes**
6	**Communicators**
7	**Knowledgeable**
8	**Efficient**
9	**Leaders**
10	**Balance**

The Ten Personal Skills of Top Sales Performers

1	**High Energy**

Our core concept in *The Essence of Selling* includes Setting Goals-Taking Actions-Monitoring Results on a continuing basis.

Selling is an action-oriented undertaking.
Action makes results happen.
Results drive more goals and more actions.
Action requires energy!

When you observe top sales professionals at work, one characteristic that jumps out at you is their energetic approach to both life and their chosen career. Why is that? Selling is hard work. To succeed in an environment

147

that requires hard work takes real energy. I do not want to insinuate that many other professions do not require equally demanding efforts, but I do want to assure you that being a top sales professional is hard work.

Recruiters of sales talent know that candidates exuding high energy levels are at an advantage when they settle into the rigors of a selling assignment. Conversely, candidates who display low energy levels are immediately in difficulty. The truth is that some people are simply blessed with high levels of energy. You will hear confessions such as, "I have always been very energetic! As a child my friends and teachers always said I was just a ball of energy!" As parents, many of us can recount stories about the child who constantly ran everybody in the household ragged from dawn to dusk. For many others, energy does not come as easily and is something that has to be developed.

Having a high energy level does not by itself make you a success in sales, but it is a quality that sets the stage for achievement!

Why High Energy Matters:
- It is the raw material of *The Essence of Selling.*
- It allows you to press on with your sales efforts when the inevitable challenges begin to mount and others begin to falter.
- Prospects sense and respond positively to energy.

"I don't know if you have the best product, or represent the most outstanding company; but if you work as hard after this sale as you have to get this order, we will be well served." Music to my ears and to yours!

"You always made us feel important, and you were always available no matter how short the notice!"

"No request was ever left unaddressed. You even showed up in the middle of a snowstorm!"

"When you talk about your product, it's with such passion and energy, we couldn't help being impressed." The sound of victory!

Selling is hard work. It requires energy. Prospects respond to energy, they respect it and gravitate to it. Why?
- People buy from people, especially from those who work energetically to earn another's business and valuable money.
- Service after the sale! They will feel comfortable that they have a BETTER chance of getting your attention because of your energy and enthusiasm.

I could give you converse examples of selling without energy, but I suspect you have already digested my message. Think about your own experiences as a consumer. I know that, more often than not, I have bought from salespeople who were energetic and passionate, all other faults aside. I hate to do business with people who seem to be sleepwalking, or upon whom I seem to be imposing when I ask them to sell me something. I think it is just plain rude to fail to make the extra effort to earn my business. Energy is contagious and powerful!

Suggestions to increase your energy levels:
- The challenge is both mental and physical. Find a diet and physical exercise program that works for you. The greater your conditioning and endurance levels, the more energy you will have.
- Make a commitment to reach your highest personal levels of energy on a continual basis, and then push the envelope even farther.
- Work on a mindset that demands, *"When I am with my prospects or customers, I will always exceed their expectations, no matter what the task or challenge. They deserve my best efforts!"*

I urge you to take advantage of the books, publications, and expert sources of information that are available on this topic. Our intent is to reinforce why high energy levels are important to your success. We will leave it to another set of experts to help you reach greater energy levels.

Do a check on your energy level frequently. When you find yourself succumbing to fatigue, remind yourself to pick up your pace. The difference between mediocre sales performance and exceptional results often comes down to making the extra effort that reserves of energy will allow you to bring forward.

Selling is Action...Action Requires Energy... Prospects Respond Positively to Energy!

2   Focus

Twenty-five years of sales experience has afforded me the opportunity to observe a lot of human nature. Let me share one observation that has always puzzled me. Many people coming into sales positions seem to believe that just the fact they are in sales will make them successful! I understand that working for the right company, with the right product, at the right time, can make achieving success appear to be intoxicatingly easy. Reality is, unfortunately, different! A significant number of people entering the selling profession will fail. In many cases, they will fail several times, before they learn how to sell, or decide to move on to another profession.

I have been told time and again by well-meaning friends and neighbors, "Salespeople have the life—money, exciting travel, expense accounts, and other people to do the really tough work! They have it made." As a capitalist society, we have embraced a myth about sales work. Those of you who are in sales know—and those embarking on selling careers are about to learn—the real truth.

Becoming a success in sales is difficult!
Reaching Top Sales Performer status is even harder!
Staying at the top is extraordinarily demanding!

You have taken the first steps to success by reading and experiencing the material *Smart Selling!* has to offer. It is the start of a quest that will engage you throughout your time in sales if you are to reach your true potential.

Achieving success starts with being focused on success:

Being one of the best has to be very important to you!
I would not presume to be able to tell you why some people have a burning desire to compete and rise to the top. That single attribute, however, can take whatever skills and talents exist and multiply them many times over. If you want success, you will have to act on achieving it. Waiting patiently for good things to happen is often a path to disappointment.

Several years ago, I was trying to fill an important sales position at our company. We had carefully drawn job specifications and descriptions for the assignment. I reluctantly interviewed a candidate who was quite inexperienced for this key position. I decided to pass on hiring this applicant, because he was just not ready for a senior sales position. Every single day for the next month he called me to ask if I would reconsider, asking if I could give advice about what he had do to persuade me to do so. How could he improve his chances for the next opportunity if this job was not available? Could I give him the job on a trial basis? I am sure you get a clear picture of someone acting to achieve something that was important. Yes, I hired him; he accepted a less senior sales position, never complained, and performed extraordinarily well. Within a year, he was promoted to the job for which he had worked so hard to be hired!

Selling is a "7 x 24 x 365" assignment.

When it matters to you, it is always on your mind! Turning your assignment into a 9 to 5 routine is the path to mediocre performance. Sometimes people ask me with real passion and occasionally hostility, *"Does this mean I am supposed to obsess on selling?"* No, this does not mean that selling becomes your whole existence. It does mean that in those quiet moments in the evening, or when you are driving in your car, or perhaps while in the shower, you take a moment to focus on current selling challenges. It is amazing the insights you will discover when you train your mind to carve out these moments in time. In fact, I believe the act of changing your environment helps you bring these discoveries out of the clutter and into your consciousness. This is the difference between a job and a profession. It also says you care enough and choose to achieve success.

You choose to make personal sacrifices.

Long hours, travel, extended periods away from home can all be part of a sales career. Spending extra effort on your prospects and territory assignments all contribute to reducing the personal time you may have available. Remember the old saying, "There is no such thing as a free lunch!" Top performers understand that success comes from sacrifice. I like to remind those who are focused on success, who do make the inevitable personal sacrifices, that you can make smart choices to reduce the difficulty of the sacrifices. Here are some suggestions: Don't make promises to your friends and family that are impossible to keep. When you do make personal commitments, zealously guard the time you have and make it quality time. Be creative.

I traveled extensively on business throughout Europe and Asia. Each summer I would make it a point to take my family on a scheduled trip. It did several things: we had quality time with each other when I was not working, and they observed first-hand how challenging and difficult a foreign sales assignment really could be. It's also important for you to discuss openly and candidly with family and friends why you are making these sacrifices. Don't be hesitant about expressing how important your career is, what you hope to achieve and the rewards you are anticipating.

The best work hard at getting even better.

No matter how talented or skilled you may be, you can always improve!

Top performers understand this reality and focus on staying at the top by working to get even better.

Several years ago, I found myself in Tokyo with a weekend layover. The hotel where I stayed was also the site of a bilingual seminar entitled, "How to make Great Presentations." It was scheduled for Saturday at 7 a.m. I realized I had struggled presenting to audiences in Japan. I needed help! A few moments after settling in a seat, I was shocked to see our company's star salesperson and our leading distributor seated in the front row. Both of these gentlemen were masters at presentations and "Top Sales Performers!" Yet, they had gotten up at 4 a.m. on a Saturday to commute to downtown Tokyo. Why? *"...to get better and stay current with new techniques!"*

One last example! I love the game of baseball. I read an article in a local paper not long ago about the star pitcher for my favorite team...a player with a long list of awards and accomplishments...in addition to a mega-million dollar contract. The reporter recounted how this star kept on video the pitch-by-pitch sequence he had thrown to *every* batter he had faced in the last five years. When he prepared to face these opponents, he would review each pitch and sequence to plan how he would attack them in their next meeting. Why? It gave him an edge to achieve success!

The best work hard at getting better!

3   Fearless

Selling is people-intensive and not for the faint of heart. We are going to discuss five thoughts that will help you overcome what I refer to as the **Fear of Failure.** These can stand in the way of your becoming a Top Performer.

Let's start by destroying a myth: "Star salespeople have no fear."

In fact, top performers suffer from the very same fears most aspiring salespeople experience. The difference is that they have learned to understand, overcome, and channel fear. They use the adrenaline rush that comes with fear to drive their personal performance. The more they experience success, the farther back in their consciousness they can push the boundaries of fear. It may always be present, but it ceases to be overwhelming because they know it can be tamed and put to work.

The Five Fear-Breaking Thoughts

1. Why not Me?

The first day I was initiated into a sales job, I attended a company sales meeting. I was in the presence of a large group of very successful and experienced sales professionals! I was certain every one in that room was wondering, "How did this guy ever get hired, and how long will he last?"

The meeting convened at an enormous conference table. My manager sat down next to me and said, *"Most of the people at this table are minimally competent at best, a few are on the right path, and one or two are stars. Learn from the best, trust in your judgment and then decide right here and now that you can and will be the best salesperson in this room."* No one at that table was eleven feet tall, no one had discovered the atom, or invented the universe or black holes; in fact, they were just ordinary people trying to survive in a difficult assignment.

I could learn the selling skills, the communications techniques, a sales methodology and product features. I could work as hard or harder, work as smart or smarter, and compete with anyone at that table. I wanted to achieve success and there was no reason I would personally accept anything less than complete success. Somebody was going to be the top salesperson. Why not me?

2. You will never know until you try!

Human nature is interesting. We are all different and yet very much alike. One of the things most people fear is the unknown. Yet the unknown, when experienced or explored, somehow becomes a little less frightening. In time, it can even become familiar, appealing, and comforting. How many people do you know will tell you? *"It was frightening at first, but once I had experienced it..."* or *"It didn't turn out as bad as I feared."*

Learning to sell, or making a first cold call, doing a major presentation or asking a senior executive for an important order, is no different than any other experience. Ask yourself what is the worst thing that can happen, acknowledge the fear, dismiss the fear, and go do it!

In time, I realized the worst thing that could happen is that someone said "No!" Occasionally, I would be embarrassed or look foolish, and in truth,

153

that did happen; but it wasn't as frequent as I had feared, and it turned out to be far from the end of the world. The alternative is to let the fear control you. When you succumb to fear, you limit your chances to experience both growth and success.

Prospecting is a problem for many salespeople. Why? At the core, the issue is fear. It is difficult to pick up a telephone or knock on a door and ask strangers to do something. Sales representatives spend incredible amounts of time avoiding, denying and generally making excuses for not prospecting. Talk to a top performer and what you will hear, time-and-time again, is that the more you prospect the easier it becomes and the better your results. The more you experience it, the more the fear is reduced, and the more your creativity emerges. Overcoming the initial fear is the first big step forward. You will never know until you try.

3. I can and will embrace change!
Every day is a new experience. Every contact with a prospect is unpredictable and different. These realities can be fear inducing. Your acceptance of change will allow you to focus your mind and sell at your best in spite of new or changing circumstances. This is the difference between sales representatives who become upset, disoriented, and then panic when something unexpected happens. Prospects are observant and respond when they see a negative reaction or panic to a question. Compare that behavior to top performers who just continue to move forward despite a new obstacle or change of agenda presented by a prospect.

I have found it useful to mentally plan my sales strategy as if a predictable path will follow, but always ask the question at each step, *"What if?"* I then reflect on the "what if" and prepare for a change. This approach helps manage the unexpected, and also reinforces the ability in my consciousness to expect the unexpected.

At a deeper level, the ability to deal with change is about control and acceptance. When we embrace change, we acknowledge that we cannot control all the events and circumstances that surround us. We can accept the unknown and unpredictable with a confidence that allows us to anticipate, respond, and react with fearlessness. We also realize we may not always get it right, but we can and will correct course and reset ourselves.

4. Does *No* really mean *No?*
Most salespeople fear the word *No!* Top Performers do not!

154

The word "no" just means "not yet."

"You have not persuaded me to agree...I am not ready to agree...I do not understand...I won't agree to this particular point." These and countless other thought processes can cause someone to say, *"No."*

Years ago, I sold a complex software product to a brand new customer. It was a long sales process and a major acquisition for this company. I asked the Executive Buyer at contract signing if he would like to purchase the other product our company marketed. His answer was a simple, "No, thanks."

> I responded to the answer with a simple question, *"Why is that?"*
> "Well, we have a similar solution that we got for free several years ago."
> *"Has it worked well for you?"*
> "No, but it was free."
> *"Okay, but if my product worked well, if it allowed you to offer your customers more new services, that may well be better than free, right?"*
> A long pause ensued. "Well, I suppose it wouldn't hurt to listen to your offer; but I want you to understand, replacing free will not be easy!"
> My response was a simple statement. I closed the second sale 90 days later!
> *"I'm not sure we can help you, but it would be valuable to both our companies if we could!"*

You disarm *No* with open-ended questions and neutral statements. If you argue, you lose. Very few people lack respect for salespeople who persist. They expect salespeople to sell!

A good friend and colleague always reminded me: *"No"* means *"No"* when I finally and politely ask my prospect, *"What you're saying is that you will never buy my product, or even consider it under any imaginable circumstances...that this product would never ever be acceptable to you?"*

The answers were often quite revealing and evenly divided between:
1. Yes, that is correct.
2. No, I don't agree with your statement.
3. Actually, I would consider your product if...

In fact, two out of three responses were not a *No* at all.

Do not fear the word "No!"

5. A rejection will never affect my self esteem.
"We have selected your competitor...Thanks for the proposal, we are going to pass on it...We are not in a position to spend any money." EVERY salesperson hears those words, no one is exempt, and it's always unpleasant.

Top professionals understand that lost opportunities are business decisions...they are rarely personal rejections.

When your prospect selects a competitor, you have failed to persuade their organization that your product, your company, and you were the best choice for them. Nothing will change that reality. However, the failure is a learning experience that can be used to make you a better competitor the next time. The goal is to reduce your defeats and increase your victories.

You must nurture a mentality that expects to win each sale, but understand you can lose any opportunity.

After a recent seminar, a participant approached me and confided that rejection was always personal for him, and was causing him to rethink pursuing a career in sales. He asked, "How can I accept losing?" I gave him some baseball wisdom. The greatest hitters, the top 1 percent in the game, may in any given year hit for a batting average of .350. Impressive, but it also says that they fail 65 percent of the time they go to the batter's box. The greatness is in the effort and belief that they will succeed each and every time, but accepting that it will not always turn out as they desire. So it is in sales. Your product, depending on your marketplace and position, may prevail in 10 percent of your at bats or 90 percent. It's your job to push that reality to the highest level of results that can be humanly achieved.

4　**Urgency and Persistence**

High Energy Levels, Focus and Fearlessness come together and lead us to Urgency and Persistence. Simply put, Urgency and Persistence require that you continue to have energy, focus and remain fearless.

The dictionary defines *urgency*, "compelling immediate action or attention; pressing;" and it defines *persistence*, "to hold firmly and steadfastly to a purpose, a state or an undertaking, despite obstacles, warnings or setbacks." The direct opposite of urgency and persistence is procrastination. I believe:

In sales, good things do not happen to those who procrastinate.

I would like to introduce you to the excuse that is used to justify procrastination. *"I build customer relationships,"* meaning, *"I am not going to push my prospects to do anything!"* The statement itself starts on solid ground. You want as a salesperson to create strong and sustainable customer relationships. In fact, if you fail at this task you will dramatically limit your success. The thought process implodes when it attempts to dismiss a simple sales reality—salespeople get paid to make things happen—not to be bystanders or gatekeepers, but to lead and compel immediate action. Why is that? Selling is about action!

Second, the statement reflects fear. Prospects expect salespeople to sell, and they reserve the right to say no to proposals, suggestions, and calls for action. Some sales practitioners overcome the fear of this word by avoiding actions that could result in a prospect saying no to them. Unfortunately, these machinations hurt their effectiveness and, in my humble opinion, do not necessarily impress your prospects. I can assure you, at the higher levels of *The Selling Pyramid,* saying no is a normal daily occurrence. Remember our previous discussion about the word no, what it really means, and then press on with selling!

The longer it takes for a prospect to reach a decision to buy your product and execute an order, the greater your exposure is to:

- A business setback, such as the loss of financial resources, or the sale of the business to new owners.
- A competitor, or new competitors, being invited to participate.
- A change of key personnel at the prospect account.
- A revision of the prospect's business model or plan, which may no longer include your product or service.

To "compel immediate action" does not mean we can or should force or manipulate people to do things, or behave in a socially obnoxious manner. It does mean that as business people we set a quick pace for the sales process and actively engage our prospects. You never want to be the reason a prospect slows down their timeframe by failing to deliver on requests they have made, or allowing the urgency of the sale to falter.

157

Every sales cycle will hit "roadblocks" and "speed bumps." Persistence is the ability to push past these obstacles and prevail. It's a quality all top performers possess. Let me give you an example of a "speed bump." Your prospect announces, *"Everybody here is concerned that your after-sales service is really second rate at best, a real problem to doing business with your company."* Wow! Where did that come from? A competitor, a customer? Is it a misguided rumor, old news, or a true statement? Are you going to overcome this issue, or fold and find another prospect? Persistence is the determination to face obstacles head on and attack them to the best of your ability. You may fail or succeed at surmounting an obstacle, but failure will not come from a lack of effort.

Salespeople who have problems with persistence struggle in a highly competitive sales marketplace. Why? The key word is competitive. The fact you have competition means you will be challenged and forced to deal with objections. Disarming objections requires large doses of persistence.

Urgency and persistence are key ingredients in the management of selling time. Everyone in sales has a limited amount of selling time (the minutes, hours or days each week, month or year) when you have access to your prospects. The more prospect interaction time you can create, the better your opportunity for success. Wasting precious time by moving at a slow pace will have a direct impact on prospect interaction time. Top performers realize the value of selling time, and that urgency and persistence are integral to getting the most out of each selling day.

"Genius is 99 percent perspiration and 1 percent inspiration. If we did all the things we are capable of doing, we would literally astound ourselves."

**Thomas Edison,
American Inventor**

5 Positive Attitudes

I will always remember reading my children *"The Little Engine That Could,"* a wonderfully entertaining children's book that held an incredible piece of wisdom for the adults fortunate enough to read this favorite bedtime story. A positive attitude portrayed from the start, "I think I can...I think

I can...I think I can" culminates with a victorious ending as the Little Blue Engine recounts, "I thought I could...I thought I could...I thought I could." *

Why is it some of us can view life with a positive attitude, show resilience when things get difficult and bounce back as positive as ever?

I have had the privilege of working with salespeople who always believed in themselves and their ability to prevail, no matter how far off plan or how bleak the immediate future appeared. In defeat, they were disappointed but never lost hope that tomorrow is another day, positive the results would be better next time around. They would regroup, figure out what to correct, and go on to achieve success. When they did experience success, they were humble, grateful, but exuded a sense that this success was not a surprise, rather the inevitable outcome of their efforts.

I have also worked with and for salespeople who were steadfast in the belief that they would fail. The failure may have been someone else's fault, or some event that was beyond their control, even an error another person was guilty of committing. It was always: a poor product, a bad territory, sales management, or company executives who had no plan or strategy. When they failed, the explanation was, "See, I knew this would happen!" Even success was greeted as a skeptic. "Let's not get carried away, we were lucky to win this order!" I am not a behavioral scientist, but I am a student of human behavior.

I believe you can decide your attitude.
I believe you become your attitude.
If you want to succeed, you will succeed!

The people you work with and sell to will sense your attitude. It will be exuded in every meeting, telephone call, or e-mail. Intentionally or not, it will make a clear statement about who you are and what you believe. Prospects want to do business with salespeople who have positive attitudes.

They are careful with whom they will risk their careers and business capital. The choice often comes down to seeking positive attitudes to trust. How could they choose otherwise? Would you buy from someone who believes he or she will fail?

*Piper, Watty, *The Little Engine That Could*, New York: Platt & Munk Publishers, 1976.

I have had very smart people ask, *"I want to be successful in sales, I have a great attitude, so why am I still waiting and failing?"* The truth is having a positive attitude is essential to achieving top performer status; however, I want you to remember, attitude by itself will not make you a success! Acting on your desire to be a top performer will! The action may require incredibly hard work, constant learning of selling skills, honing communication skills, embracing a sales methodology, and learning from the things you do well and the failures you experience.

A positive attitude will sustain you while the skills you need for top performer status develop through diligence and hard work.

6 · Communicators

Top Performers have learned with whom to communicate, what to communicate, and when to deliver their sales proposal. They have polished these skills as they have progressed in their professional and personal growth. When you observe them selling, the communication they carry forward all seems so easy and natural. That is because for them it truly is!

Great sales communicators are not born, they are trained. Granted, for some the training is more intuitive than for others; but it is a learned skill, no different from other professional skills. I want you to think about this: Savvy communications pay dividends from the very first day you act to improve your skills, and will continue to provide benefits, both immediate and long-term, as you become more proficient!

(Much of the material here is drawn from Chapter 3, The Selling Pyramid*; it can be found there in greater detail.)*

With whom do Top Performers communicate?
I learned quickly in my sales career that I could either communicate directly with the top executives at my prospect accounts or:

- I could rely on someone else to do it in my stead.
- I could rely on my competitors to mention me.
- I could just ignore the top executives.
  ...the bad, the very bad, and the very worst!

So why do thousands of salespeople choose one of these options every single selling day? I suppose there are a variety of reasons—fear, ignorance, or a 'whatever' attitude. I do not want you to make the same mistake. One thing I can assure you, top performers do not make this mistake!

Learning to sell to Cs and Executive Buyers is essential to your selling career. The good news is that this is a sales-friendly audience because many of these executives or business owners have been salespeople in their careers. They understand that you may have something they want and need. Remember, these executives prosper when their business is successful. They are driven and focused on achieving their goals; and they have the unique power to act, spend money, and commit their organizations. Your challenge is to persuade them to act!

Does this mean you should stop selling to Evaluators and Recommenders? No, but you need to understand they have a role and needs that are different from the executives who are your ultimate target audience. Work with Evaluators and Recommenders, build relationships, but do not expect them to buy your product or to sell it internally for you! Don't make them the focal point of your selling efforts.

What do Top Performers communicate?

The answer is incredibly simple and straightforward! They communicate to Executive Buyers what this audience clearly wants and needs to make them successful!

How does your product make it possible for them to grow their sales and/or reduce expenses?

Top Performers have learned to communicate by:
- Focusing on the prospect by listening intently and actively. They convey to the prospect that they value the time being spent with this "special" person, whom they desire to make more successful.
- Asking prospects important questions that are:
  1. Open-ended
  2. Clarifying and reinforcing
  3. Focused on the big picture issue of Growing Sales/ Reducing Expenses
- Discovering the Prospects':
  1. Needs
  2. Wants
- Then revealing, "I understand! Here is how my product can help you grow revenues/reduce expenses."

They avoid three fatal communication errors:
- I do not have the time or interest to find out what you need.
- I can't listen because I am too busy talking about my product.
- I am worried about my success, not yours.

When should you deliver your sales proposal?

You could deliver your proposal before you know anything about your prospects' needs. "Here is what I would like to sell you!" Perhaps you could say, "I am not sure what you need, but here is my product anyway!" My personal favorite is, "I can reduce the list price of my product by 30 percent, now let me tell you about it." Again, this happens every selling day.

Top Performers understand that the power of a sales proposal is greatly enhanced when you qualify a prospect, explore and comprehend their needs, develop a mutual understanding of how your solution can meet those needs, and then propose your product—which is exactly what they are used to doing!

This activity includes engaging the Executive Buyers at your prospect account early in the sales cycle. They remind the top executives that they may or may not be able to help the account grow revenue or reduce expenses. They seek permission to explore whether they can deliver value, and thus the product evaluation process is underway. They keep communicating with the Executive Buyers through updates on the progress of the sales process.

Chapter 4, *The Business Sales Methodology,* explores when and how to deliver sales proposals in much greater detail.

Communications:
- **Expressing oneself in such a way that one
  is readily and clearly understood**
- **Learning to Listen...Asking to Learn**
- **Focusing on the other person**

7   Knowledgeable

In medieval Europe, merchants traveling from city to city were the major source of news and information from the outside world. While much has changed in the 21st century, people still enjoy hearing news about their industry and competitors from salespeople, along with details about new products and business trends.

Nothing is more difficult than competing with a skilled salesman or woman, who is also a business person with industry knowledge and product expertise! We often refer to these people as Top Performers!

If you intend to be successful in selling products to other business enterprises, learn how trade is conducted, what current issues are in play, and what trends are on the horizon. Businessmen and women like to work with astute people. They feel comfortable with those who understand their specific industry and business in general. Reading industry newspapers and targeted publications will give you a knowledgeable background in commerce.

Learning specifics about the industry you work in and sell to is essential. If your company is a plastics manufacturer, study all phases of the industry. If your customers are large retailers in home improvement, immerse yourself in news about that marketplace. Top Performers understand the importance of being viewed as industry insiders.

Executives view as partners and intelligence providers salespeople who are comfortable discussing the business issues which affect their company and marketplace.

Reading books and trade publications, attending industry trade events, finding mentors, as well as taking courses, can make you an expert quicker than you may initially have believed possible. It takes work, but it will set you apart from your competitors. The goal is to convince the executives at your prospect accounts that you understand their business environment, can be a source of information and add value; in short, worth the meeting time.

Why does this matter? You establish credibility as you enter into a product discussion, and exploration of a value proposition. It also sends a message that you are serious about making your prospect successful. Let's ask the question, *"As opposed to what?"* Given the choice of buying from someone who knows nothing about your business or trusting your business to someone with serious knowledge of your environment and industry, what would you choose to do? I think we both know the answer!

Why is product knowledge paramount? How can I add value to my prospect's business if I don't know why or how my product meets their needs? Top performers know their products inside and out. They also know when to ask for help in determining how their product best adds value.

Becoming an expert on the product you sell can be a simple assignment or extraordinarily difficult. Much will depend on your business model. For example, if you sell one product, complex or not, you can almost always become an expert. However, suppose you are responsible for ten complex and diverse products. The challenge of amassing that much expertise may be overwhelming. If you have a number of products you sell, you want to become knowledgeable about each offering at least to the point where you can comfortably articulate key solution benefits to an executive audience.

Other experts in your organization should manage functional product details or engineering specifications. What you must clearly understand is "when and how" to access the assistance you will require. Experience has taught me this is an important issue that every company selling complex products needs to carefully explore and resolve. I have witnessed far too many failures that were the result of complete organizations, including their sales and marketing teams, not understanding how their complex product could be explained to prospect audiences.

Countless interviews of Executive Buyers at prospect accounts have reinforced for me that this crucial audience has great respect for sales professionals who display business, industry and product expertise. They also have complete contempt for salespeople who fail in all three categories. Top professionals understand this simple reality and use it to their advantage.

8 | Efficient

"Selling Time" is the great equalizer. Have you ever found yourself thinking, "If only I could have made one more sale this week, this month, or this year? That additional sale would have allowed me to become the salesperson of the year, or to buy the new car I wanted."

Top Performers develop a passion for protecting and extending the amount of selling time available to them. They understand that more selling time equates to more opportunity for success and achievement. Unfortunately, it is not available in unlimited quantities—that's why it's so valuable!

You can create selling time by:
- Removing administrative and operational tasks from your selling day
- Reserving your selling hours for selling to real prospects that are qualified to buy your product

I recently spent time with a salesperson who was lamenting the lack of time available to spend with his prospects. He was struggling to make plan and growing frustrated. We quickly agreed that his prospects were accessible Monday through Friday for about 10 hours each day either in person or by telephone. Fifty selling hours each week. I asked him to take me through how he spent his time this last week. Here is a quick overview of the conversation:

"Monday was spent doing sales reports, forecasts and expense accounts. I also used the day to plan my week and made some telephone calls to colleagues in marketing and sales support." *(In fact, the whole selling day was lost doing administrative work, 20 percent of the week gone! All this could have been accomplished after hours, on weekends or with some e-mails.)*

"Tuesday morning I drove to a prospect meeting scheduled for 3 p.m. It was a 4-hour drive, so I made some phone calls from the car to other prospects. *(My estimate was that half the day was spent selling, another 10 percent of the week gone. Remember, he could have traveled in the evening hours.)* At this point, this colleague stopped and said, "I am wasting a lot of selling time!"

Top performers understand that selling hours are not best utilized on administrative tasks. I hope you will too!

Take a weekly calendar and do the same exercise for yourself. Keep asking the question, "How can I do this task without impacting my selling hours?"

Actions to conserve your real selling time:

- **Fire the "Tire Kickers" and "Professional Lookers."**
  Every salesperson has these characters in their portfolio of prospects. Many of them are well-meaning and charming people—the consultants who represent unnamed companies that are potentially interested in your product, the business partners who need help on some big future opportunity; suspects who may have an interest if only they had more information—they just need you to educate them about your product, the industry, your competitors, etc. Unfortunately, as a group, they steal your selling time. Smart selling says, *"I either conclude you are a qualified prospect, or I have to stop using my selling time on you."* Try finding another person in your company to assist them or move their requests to after hours.

- **Qualify and re-qualify your prospects.**
  Similar to "Tire Kickers" except you become the real cause of this problem. These are prospects that either never were qualified or have subsequently disqualified themselves, but you refuse to let go. They are now "suspects" at best. Someone will usually ask, "How about persistence? I am suppose to overcome obstacles, right?" That's correct, but I reserve persistence for prospects that are challenged. Suspects are off the table until I can get them re-qualified. For example, if an account has lost budget funding or is now financially distressed, continuing to call on them and asking for an order is not a good use of selling time. I have seen too many salespeople fail because it is easier to hold on to these accounts than to let go and find replacement opportunities. Difficult to do, but necessary!

166

- **Delegate the routine.**
  Top performers understand the power of leverage. Having an assistant or an ambitious co-worker get some of the routine tasks out from under you is smart. Let someone else confirm your appointments, return non-essential phone or e-mail messages to answer simple questions. Remember, the work you may consider routine and time consuming may be someone else's chance to do something new and challenging.

Take a time management course or read a book on this topic. Your time will be well spent and the rewards significant.

9 Leaders

What is sales leadership? It's the act of directing your prospects through a discovery process that leads them to conclude your product best provides the value they need and must acquire.

Experience has taught me that prospects want:
- To be respected, listened to and treated as special.
- To have their needs come first always.
- To be successful!

Top performers understand this reality and focus on making sure they take care of their prospect's needs. They are truly customer-focused! Top performers rise above the mediocre in understanding several other issues about prospects:
- They seek direction and respect action.
- They want to do business with *leaders*.
- They want value from their purchases.

Have you ever been so frustrated in trying to make a purchase that you find yourself saying, "I need some help! I want to deal with your best salesperson and I want that person now!" I certainly have. I was asking for direction, action and leadership!

Several years ago, a top performer was asked by an early stage suspect to provide them with her ten best reference accounts so they could decide if they had any interest in her product. "Just give us the names, titles and telephone numbers and we'll take it from there!" The suspect had very little knowledge about her solution and had not even been qualified as a

167

real prospect. They had made a legitimate request and wanted attention. The easy solution would have been to give the suspect what they had requested, be customer-focused, assume they knew what they wanted—or is that a mistake? Here is how our "top performer" responded:

> *"This is an unusual request. I want to best serve your interest. Could we discuss why you want to take this approach?"*
>
> "My boss told me to do it this way," replied the suspect.
>
> *"I understand, let me tell you why most of our customers choose to wait to call our references. They want to have more information about our product so the calls are more meaningful and productive. They hate to waste their own time, and candidly, the time of our reference accounts until they are fully prepared."*
>
> The suspect responded positively because the comments made perfect sense.
>
> Our star performer closed with, *"I would be glad to meet with you and your boss, get a better understanding of your needs, and explain our position. I am sure I could arrange and participate in a call to a reference account with the understanding that you are really just getting started in exploring the value of our product if that would be helpful?"* Direction, action and leadership!

An "expert" once told me that sales is easy if you just befriend the prospect, give them what they ask, keep asking for the order, and above all else, keep smiling. I agree that this advice may make a career in sales seem easy, but it comes from a school of thought that has long since ceased to be meaningful. I have often wondered what that "expert" would do with suspects that were unsure or simply did not know what they needed.

Sales leadership is also focused on being certain that the product you sell to your prospects will meet their needs. Top performers understand that selling anything to anybody is not a path to long-term sustainable success. Does that mean every one of your customers will be 100 percent plus delighted with your product? Unfortunately, it does not. What you do want is to be 100 percent certain that all your customers feel they were treated fairly and honestly during the sales process.

Sales leadership is also careful in embracing the ever-popular fads of simple "tips and tricks" which often promise easy answers to difficult selling challenges. Shortcuts will not replace either fundamental selling skills or personal steps to top sales performance. I believe valuable information can be found in almost any concept, and that part of professional growth is to be open and eager to embrace and explore new ideas and concepts. Not long ago I read some material that espoused "cold calls" as a dead concept that was not worth the time. Interesting thought! However, I can assure you that top performers would not immediately call a halt to their prospecting, or decide not to continue to hone this very fundamental skill.

Our society, economic climate and business environment are becoming ever more dynamic, complex and competitive. Sales leadership is still very much in demand and always will be! Top performers understand the premium that is placed on it and the rewards that come from exercising leadership.

10 Balance

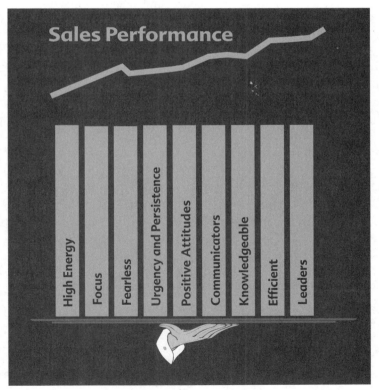

"Balance" is a strength which allows Top Performers to both achieve and maintain their superior level of performance. In their personal and professional growth, they've reached a sustained level of competency.

169

Their expertise encompasses:

- Sales skills.
- Communications skills.
- A sales methodology.
- Product, industry and business knowledge.
- The motivation to excel.

When you achieve "Balance," you have developed significant skill sets in each of these qualities. You may possess extraordinary skills in one category and ongoing challenges in another—but each of these essential skill sets has enough depth to support top performance. The sum of these strengths is a broadly based competency all top performers exhibit and convey to their prospects, customers, and managers.

Conversely, when you are out of balance, your deficiency in one or several of our disciplines compromises your overall performance. For example, salespeople who come from engineering or other technical assignments, or who have spent time in product marketing or sales support, have strong product and industry backgrounds. However, they often initially struggle with communication and selling skills. It does not matter what your challenge is as much as it matters that you recognize the issues impeding your achievement. Then, act to strengthen them.

Creativity can help you overcome challenges. I struggled in several selling assignments with engineering-intense products I had to sell to be a top performer. Try as I did, some of the concepts were beyond my grasp. In a moment of creativity, I managed to convince our company's CEO to team me with a junior engineer (who was scheduled to be laid off) for six months to see if that would boost my performance. Within that time, my sales results exploded. I became the top salesperson in our company and the increase in sales more than paid for my overjoyed partner's compensation. After months of daily schooling, he finally succeeded in getting me up to speed on what had been some very foreign concepts. Many learning resources are available to help you improve your selling and communications skills, or increase your motivation. In fact, you have already taken a major step forward with this book. Just keep working at it!

Occasionally, people will tell me that despite their best efforts they were unable to get enough improvement in a particular discipline. I have always been suspicious about the "I just could not" argument. I believe anyone can achieve enough strength in each of our key components if they truly want to succeed. The challenges can be difficult, but they can be overcome. It is seductive in sales to look at colleagues around you who have failed and get comfortable with failing yourself. I would argue it is just as easy to admire the Top Performers and ask, "Why not me?"

Think of Balance as a recipe for achieving top performance.
Work on getting each ingredient right...
and you will reach your goals!

Final Reminders!

The commitment to achieve extraordinary results starts with a realization that we each have within us the ability to reach far beyond the ordinary. The personal decision to take the first steps to extending our achievements comes to each of us through different circumstances and life experiences.

The Ten Personal Skills of Top Performers is available to help you on your personal quest for excellence when you are ready to undertake the journey. These personal skills will greatly multiply the power and effectiveness of the fundamental sales skills and disciplines we have discussed. They can also compensate for both selling, communications or other business skills which you have not yet fully developed or experienced early in your sales career.

I would like to encourage you to give each skill careful consideration.

Self-Assessment Chart

Date: _____

		Poor					Very strong			
1	High Energy									
2	Focus									
3	Fearless									
4	Urgency and Persistence									
5	Positive Attitudes									
6	Communicators									
7	Knowledgeable									
8	Efficient									
9	Leaders									
10	Balance									

Monitor your performance and track your progress!

Test Your Knowledge

Ten Skills Of Top Sales Performers

1. If you make quota for one year, you will always be known as a Top Performer.　　True/False

2. Selling is an action-oriented undertaking and action has very little impact on results because it requires energy.　　True/False

3. Once you have become successful in sales your momentum will allow you to ease off and coast to more success.　　True/False

4. Some "Fear-Breaking Thoughts" include:　　_____,_____,_____
    A. Why not me?
    B. You'll never know until you try!
    C. I can and will avoid change!
    D. Does NO really mean NO?

5. In sales, "Good things happen to those who procrastinate!"　　True/False

6. Communications is built around
    A. Learning to Listen..Asking to _____

    B. Focusing on the _____

7. Selling Time is the great equalizer!　　True/False

8. List The Ten Personal Skills of Top Performers:

    _____　　_____

    _____　　_____

    _____　　_____

    _____　　_____

    _____　　_____

9. Balance is important because it allows you to do many different tasks at once.　　True/False

10. Why is a positive attitude important?_____

_____

CHAPTER 7

How to Get and Keep Your First Sales Job

Roadmap Notes

To Salespeople

There are always a robust number of sales positions in every conceivable economic environment. Why? Every business needs sales revenue to survive, grow and prosper. We will show you how to find the position you want, with the company that best fits your needs, and how to persuade a hiring manager to give you that all-important first opportunity.

To Managers

Hire the right sales team members and life is good; select the wrong candidates and your ability to succeed is extremely limited. Hiring managers have the responsibility to find contributors and to nurture their success. In the end, you are fully accountable for those selections and the results they deliver. The first-time sales recruit is, in many ways, simpler and more effective than recruiting the expensive and hard-to-find professional.

To Business Owners

A business rises or falls on the effectiveness of its sales efforts. Generating revenue is the ultimate test. Every hiring mistake costs both capital and valuable time. You may get second chances, but they are expensive! Hiring entry-level sales staff is a reality and economic necessity that can provide real dividends.

How to Get Your First Sales Job

Finding your first sales job requires research, persistence and good interviewing skills. Throw in a bit of career planning and you are off and running. Sounds simple enough?

Who do I want to sell for?

The easy answer is, "Who cares? I just want a job. In fact, any sales job will do!" The problem with this approach is the risk of lost time and opportunity. You may not get any credit for working in a sales assignment far from your chosen field. Working in sales at a local department store may not help you get a coveted pharmaceutical sales position. In fact, it may set you back! A hiring manager will rightfully ask why you chose to take such a position. The more "temporary" positions you have, the more difficult it becomes to land a serious opportunity. Focus on what you want and do not compromise.

Not every business is prepared to support entry-level sales practitioners. Some companies may not be learning friendly; their business model may require skills that come from years of specialized experience. I want you to get your career on track quickly and to maximize the learning experiences that are available. You can accomplish this by taking four simple actions.

1. **Decide on a career path that appeals to you.**
   If you want to work in the medical field, pursue positions that are part of that broad industry. Your choice may be driven by your education, a family member or a genuine fascination. Statistics show you will likely have three or more careers in your lifetime, so it's perfectly okay to explore one field of interest, only to discover years later something else really attracts your attention. The key point is to pick a starting point which meets your career goals.

2. **Research the outstanding employers in the field you have chosen.**
   Countless databases and listing services will allow you to quickly build a list of potential employers. You can sort the lists by any criteria important to your search. Give careful consideration to those employers who have reputations for offering the best training programs. Determine which are the growth companies. What kind of reputations do key industry employers enjoy? Do you want to work at

177

a larger well-established business or a smaller entrepreneurial player? Who is advertising to hire and who is not? These and other questions will help you target which employers you want to approach. Good research and homework will pay real dividends.

3. Network!

Find recent graduates, friends, relatives or acquaintances and ask them to share their experiences in searching for sales positions. What have they learned that can be valuable to your search? What was their experience with specific companies? Can they introduce you to hiring managers or other business people? The goal is to get a personal referral from someone to an individual who can help you with your job search. The more networking you do, the greater the number of opportunities you will be exposed to.

4. Revisit our discussion in Chapter 1 about the four types of salespeople and what type of jobs best fit your profile.

The profiles give you the opportunity to reflect on how you deal with two fundamental challenges—the ability to accept change/risk and the willingness to engage in action-oriented tasks. Alligning your new job to your profile will increase your chances of success!

Having decided where you want to start your selling career and who the target companies are for employment, you are ready for the second step.

How to get an interview

Two key issues we are going to discuss—how to get an interview and how to make the interview a successful experience. There is a skill set to interviewing that is going to sound very familiar. Interviews are better known as selling! The product you are going to sell is one you are very familiar with and best qualified to represent...yourself!

In Chapter 6, we discussed persistence and fearlessness, personal qualities which will be very helpful as you embark on this next step. I am going to share with you a simple action you can take to get a sales interview at almost any business. Call the company and ask to speak to the person in charge of sales. Introduce yourself and tell the sales manager, *"I am considering a career in sales and I would like your advice about getting my first job. Can I get 15 minutes of your time?"*

If you are working on the second or third sales assignment, try this approach, *"I am early on in my sales career and I would like to get your advice*

178

about advancing to the next sales assignment." The sales executive may ask how you got his or her name. Your reply is, *"I have researched several outstanding companies in your field and your company keeps coming up as a leader,"* or *"I was referred by..."*

The message you have delivered is powerful! It says you have done your homework, you are prospecting, and you have the personal persistence and fearlessness any sales manager wants in a recruit. Close for an appointment! Ask about today, tomorrow, next week or whenever you can get on the executive's calendar. Persistent and fearless!

Since I have told you what to do, I also will tell you what not to do. Do not call the Human Resources Department and ask if they have sales positions available. Why? "Gatekeepers" do not buy products. Do not send unsolicited resumes, they will be promptly circulated, filed and lost for all eternity, while you sit and wait for a response. People buy from people, resumes do not sell themselves!

How can I tell if a position is available? The vast majority of sales managers always have positions available! Sometimes the openings are immediate; on other occasions, they are future opportunities. They are constantly recruiting because of several business facts—salespeople resign and need to be replaced quickly; staffing plans are adjusted to reflect either current or projected business trends; and finally, someone is failing to perform and the situation needs to be resolved. My advice is: focus on a strong interview performance and the opening will take care of itself. We discussed earlier why you always want to be a top performer if you are in sales. Conversely, you never want to be the bottom-ranked producer on your sales team because you are always one outstanding interview away from being replaced!

Get great interview results!

Think of the interview as a sales call, which is exactly what it is. Since you have spent the last several days reading *Smart Selling!* you should be confident and ready. There are three important interview issues:
- First impressions count.
- Listen and learn is essential.
- Focus on the interview and your goal.

The vast majority of interviews are over within 5 to 10 minutes! Why? First impressions do not take long to form. The final hiring decision may take several more meetings, but most hiring managers will quickly determine if they are comfortable with you as a candidate. The question every sales manager will ask himself or herself is, "Would I buy from this person?"

You can influence the first impression you make by being sure you are dressed appropriately. Don't show up in casual clothes to interview at a buttoned-down financial institution. If you are uncertain about the dress code for your interview, ask a friend or visit the business around lunch hour just to get a sense of attire. When in doubt, overdress. Bright-eyed, energetic and positive attitudes go a long way to a favorable reception. No interviewer will appreciate a tired disheveled candidate who seems to be sleepwalking. Bring your personality to the interview. Conventional wisdom is that if you don't put your best on display at an interview, it will just get worse after you are hired.

The interview is an opportunity to learn about the company you are considering. It is a compliment to your prospective employer to display your listening skills, ask open-ended questions, and absorb as much information as possible—just as you will do on sales calls. If you monopolize the conversation, red flags will begin to go up. If the questions you ask are well thought-out and intelligent, you will get high marks. Start asking about issues that are viewed as secondary or inappropriate and the interviewer will begin to disengage.

I can recall an interview in which the very first question the candidate raised was: "How often do you fire salespeople?" followed by, "Will commission payments be made as promised?" The negativity coming from the candidate was very palpable. My first thought was: "Great, I have not even hired you and you are already concerned with failing." Not a favorable impression! Use Goals-Actions-Results to set a realistic objective for the interview. You may decide your goal is to get acquainted with the hiring manager, learn a little about the business, tell the interviewer why you would make an excellent hire, and as a result, be invited back for a second more comprehensive meeting.

Focus your attention on the interview; being distracted or appearing disorganized is a fatal mistake. I had a candidate take a cell phone call during an interview. Does that sound like someone who is focused? Sales managers will assume that if you are nervous or fidgety you will perform exactly the same in front of prospects and customers. They might conclude, "If you are intimidated by me, wait until you get confronted by a difficult customer." I mentioned personality before; it is important not to be so guarded or controlled that the interviewer does not get a chance to see your individuality.

Finally, you want the interview to help build a personal relationship. I used the word relationship rather than friendship. Your objective is to be hired, which is a mutually beneficial business transaction. Interviewers are not looking for new best friends, but they do want to be certain you can work as a part of a selling team.

Winning the Job

The bottom line on getting hired was best summarized in a previous discussion. "You sell people what they need and want." Sales managers need people who can deliver results. Convince your prospective employer you understand this reality, are anxious to prove you can succeed, and the rest of the challenge falls into place. Here's the winning message you must get comfortable expressing:

- I want the opportunity to sell for this company.
- I view sales as a part of my career plan.
- What I lack in experience, I will overcome with dedication and hard work.
- Learning and personal growth are important to me.
- I expect to be held accountable and rewarded when I deliver results!

When the inevitable phrase, "Tell me about yourself!" is asked, most candidates will respond with a biography or talk about hobbies, all of which is fine. But, I want you to select several of *The 10 Personal Skills of Top Performers* and discuss the impact they have made in your life. For example, "I always remind myself how important High Energy is to being successful in sales. I know my commitment to working energetically for my prospects will be appreciated." "I am focused on being a top sales performer. I realize it will require personal sacrifices; but, I am committed to being an exceptional producer."

1	High Energy
2	Focus
3	Fearless
4	Urgency and Persistence
5	Positive Attitudes
6	Communicators
7	Knowledgeable
8	Efficient
9	Leaders
10	Balance

Every sales manager understands that business is about taking risks. The decision to hire new sales practitioners is always perilous. The message I want you to present now will make the decision to hire you far more comforting.

Should I negotiate the terms of my employment?

Two schools of thought: one approach is to impress your manager with a desire to use your negotiation skills; it will set the tone for your behavior with prospects. The second approach is to accept the standard sales compensation package and get to work as quickly as possible.

I believe experienced professionals should negotiate without any qualms. Rookie salespeople are better served by asking for several small concessions, few of which may be agreed to, and focusing on learning and demonstrating they can deliver results. Concessions will ultimately come from the delivery of sales results. Your first priority is to get the job! Inexperienced negotiators can quickly appear to be greedy and focused on the wrong issues.

I can clearly recall a candidate trying to negotiate a fixed salary rather than accept a standard salary plus commission plan. The discussion cost the candidate an employment offer because we were committed to all sales positions being incentive-based. The philosophy was ingrained in our business and was designed to reward performance. In our company, you produced and prospered or you moved on! The continual focus on guarantees left an impression of a candidate who was uncomfortable with being accountable for producing sales.

Should I accept the first employment offer I receive?

Once you are offered a sales position, you will have to decide if it is an opportunity you want to accept. Do not feel obligated to take the first offer you receive. Forget the "any job is better than no job" mentality, and focus your search on taking only positions which include working for a sales manager committed to your success and a company with a solid business record. You still have a bit more homework and research to finish.

The manager you work for will have an enormous impact on your ability to learn and ultimately produce results. Is he or she interested in helping you to succeed, or indifferent? Ask these questions:

- Why is it important to you that I succeed?
- How will you help me reach my potential?
- Tell me about the last new recruits you hired?
- Can I meet one of these new salespeople?

Sales managers who are delighted by and comfortable with discussing these questions are winners; those who get defensive or flustered are problems waiting to happen. Work for managers who are proud of the success achieved by the salespeople they have hired and nurtured. Stay away from those who are all about themselves and indifferent to growing talent in their organization.

Two weeks into my first sales assignment, a new VP of Sales was named. I did not work for "Fred" but his impact was quickly felt throughout the business. My sales manager was clearly alarmed and I soon found out why! "Fred" did not like salespeople; in fact, he had complete and utter contempt for each and every person in the organization. He had no interest in creating a environment that was success-oriented or growing a sales team. "Fred" wanted nothing more than to keep his job. His daily routine was to badger and second guess everything everybody did. No accomplishment went unpunished! The damage he inflicted on the business was real; mercifully his reign lasted only several months. A lot of talented new sales recruits and seasoned professionals resigned along the way. The "Freds" of the world are very real! Do your best to avoid them.

First sales positions are difficult enough. Do not volunteer to complicate your learning experience by working for a business that is struggling. Leave working at challenged business organizations for experienced sales professionals. Choose a well-managed company for that first assignment.

How do I keep my sales position?

It is not unusual to hear salespeople reflect on how difficult it can be to achieve sustainable success. Often, keeping a sales position is far more of a challenge than landing the job. Sales managers and business owners need sales revenue for their companies to exist. Recruits who can deliver sales are rewarded; those who fail to produce are dismissed. In many organizations, the time between an employment offer and a termination can seem agonizingly short. What have you sold today? That's a question which has a real and serious undertone. You were given a sales position because someone was willing to believe you had the ability to be a successful contributor. Now, it becomes your responsibility to live up to their expectations as well as your own. I have observed early-stage sales careers and have seen how they get derailed. The good news is that most of these issues can be avoided. The single most important piece of advice I can impart is:

The bottom line in sales is to deliver measurable results!

Measurable results are the report card of your performance. They will be referred to as quota, gross sales per period, or revenue contributed—black and white criteria, with very little room for misinterpretation. This phenomenon is what makes sales so different from most other business assignments. You will know, as well as everyone else, if you have achieved those expectations. There are few gray areas or interpretation issues.

Smart Selling! Your Roadmap to Becoming a Top Performer has been created to do exactly what the title purports. Follow this roadmap and the challenge of producing measurable results can be mastered!

Roadblocks to early sales career success

1. I got the job!

The employment offer is only an invitation to compete. It is very common for new salespeople to be lulled into equating the success of being selected for a sales assignment as success itself! Congratulate yourself for being hired, but remember, "Now the real work begins!" The quicker you engage in your new assignment, the faster you will be able to apply what you have learned, and start producing sales. The first observation your sales manager will make is how quickly you engage!

2. No mistakes here!

Everybody expects new salespeople to make mistakes. They also expect you to learn from your errors. Asking for help, and admitting you need guidance, is healthy. Refusing assistance and ignoring your mistakes, or worse yet—blaming others when the inevitable errors occur—is a red flag. I always respected the honesty of "Yes, as dumb as it was, I did it!" followed by "The best news is I have learned my lesson and will try not to make that mistake again!"

3. This is really easy!

Early success is not a guarantee of anything! In fact, early success can lead to early failure. Why? A quick story about a scenario I have observed more times than I care to recount.

William was a talented and highly regarded hire—smart, good communications skills and gifted with a likable nature. The first quarter he was in sales, he exceeded his numbers. We all sang his praises. He did even better in his second quarter. The owner of our company personally anointed him as a star in the making. Fast forward three years. I bumped into William waiting in a hotel check-in line. He told me he was no longer in sales. In fact, he had been replaced about 18 months into his career. "They fired me and, in hindsight, they were right! I lost my focus when the successes came so quickly. I started taking days off. Then, I found excuses not to work on Monday mornings or Friday afternoons. It was summer, then it was the holidays—all great reasons to relax and enjoy! The commission checks stopped arriving each month. Prospecting became a burden until I had no prospects, and it all crashed down."

I can empathize with this reality because I narrowly missed this roadblock in my own sales career. I was fortunate enough to have a mentor who lectured me loudly and often about "selling scared." He would remind me that despite one or two years of success, I really knew much less than I

185

believed. The day you lose your edge and stop doing all the success-sustaining tasks that are so time consuming and difficult is the day you stop "selling scared." When your achievements and accolades become more important than the sales work that made them possible, you start down the path to mediocrity or worse.

4. It's only an interim job!

Yes, but it is an assignment at which you have to succeed! Aspiring management candidates are often tested in sales as a first step in their employer's training program. Sometimes a sales position is the only opportunity available at a company you want to join. However, it's always a mistake to focus on your next assignment at the expense of the current one. Here is a conversation I recently overheard at a social event:

"I wanted to be an editor at a major publishing house after graduation. I was ecstatic to be accepted into the management training program of a well-known publisher. After several days of company orientation, I was given the name of my new boss and told to report the next morning for my first assignment. I was shocked to discover he was a regional sales manager in the textbook division. My goal was to become an editor! The sales manager explained sympathetically, I could be an editor, or not! That position would be available *after* I demonstrated during the next several years my proficiency at selling textbooks to every university in three midwestern states. He handed me the keys to my company car and requested I let him know when the annual mileage approached 100,000 so he could get me a replacement vehicle. That way I would not lose any valuable road time. I did become an editor eventually...but only after selling a lot of books and passing several other tests of my ability along the way. To this day, I still hold vivid images of every single interstate hotel and diner within that three-state territory."

Failed salespeople do not usually get promoted to marketing, product management, or anything else. They may be transferred to other entry-level positions, but the record of failure goes with them.

5. This doesn't count!

"I intend to quickly secure a better sales job!" There is nothing unusual about this statement. The roadblock surfaces when a second part of the statement is the declaration, "Since I am looking for another job, I do not have to exert my best efforts!" Sloppy work leads to bad selling habits, which can require time to correct. Yesterday's failure can become an obstacle when you apply for the subsequent job you really want. Sales managers understand failures, but not when they come with a "did not try

186

very hard" reference. Commit to succeeding at every job you take; it's smart career management.

There are other roadblocks that can derail early-stage careers, many of which involve people struggling with personal issues. It is exceedingly difficult to focus on a sales position when your life is in turmoil. I learned long ago, as a manager, to accept the fact that, despite my best efforts, not every salesperson I hired would succeed, often for reasons beyond the workplace. It makes the failures due to roadblocks even more difficult to accept.

What happens if I fail at a sales assignment?
You will experience failure in a sales assignment unless you are incredibly fortunate or extraordinarily talented, just as most of us will stumble at some point in our lives. Failure may come early in your sales career or in mid-career; it may occur just once or several times. How often have you read about successful, well-known entrepreneurs who failed at business ventures time after time before they got it right?

Failing can be a humbling, but incredibly rich, learning experience. It is totally your choice to either learn from the experience or be overwhelmed. The wrong type of sales assignment for your personality is a common source of failure, as is working for or starting a business which fails to survive. It is not uncommon for the product or service which you commit to sell to simply be rejected by its target market. I have sold for businesses that just could not get their product to work as it was designed and marketed. The point is—business failures are common and very hard to avoid. The more risk you are willing to take, the more you will encounter disappointing results. You will also learn to savor the inevitable successes I know you will achieve.

When you encounter a business failure or are dismissed from a sales assignment, ask yourself:

- What could I have done differently?
- What warning signs should I have seen and how should I have responded?
- Did I make selling errors?
- How can I avoid making these selling mistakes in the future?
- Finally, what value can I take from this experience? Then, move on to the next success, a little wiser and better prepared!

How to Get and Keep Your First Sales Job is a powerful summary which cuts to the quick. Getting a sales job is an act of selling! Keeping it comes from delivering measurable results! Real selling skills matter; they will get you hired and allow you to become a top performer. You are now prepared to put your real selling skills to work!

The Last Words...

I would like to thank you for allowing me to serve as your guide as you learn the skills that compose *Smart Selling!* I hope you will agree that the title says it all: *Your Roadmap to Becoming a Top Performer.* This work is the sum of 25 years of real-life selling experiences. I personally wish I could have read a similar book at the start of my own sales career...I suspect the road would have had fewer potholes. When you are challenged by new issues and responsibilities, this text will help! The path to reaching your goal of top performance is in front of you. Here are some final observations.

Real Selling Skills Matter in a hyper-competitive world!
The search for revenue growth has become paramount for all business entities. Salespeople who can deliver results will always be in great demand.

The best always work hard at getting better.
Learning is a lifelong journey. When you stop working at improving your sales skills, you begin the descent to mediocrity. Far too many people settle for one year of experience, repeated again and again.

Anticipate the bumps along the way.
Some sales assignments will not work, no matter how skilled and dedicated you may be. The wisdom is in knowing you have done your best and accepting that it may not always meet your expectations.

Change is a constant.
Be prepared to respond to change. The economic order of the 21st century is volatile and will get more volatile. Enjoy your successes where you find them and remain vigilant to complacency. Today's reality is that you will not find one business, one sales position or one career that will encompass your working life.

The shortcuts to success are enticing but seldom valuable.
We live in a society that is gratification-oriented and impatient. It is easy to be enticed to run before you have mastered walking. You have now learned fundamental selling skills, it is time to practice putting them to work. Keep an open mind about the countless expert selling tips and tricks which promise startling improvements. Evaluate them against the fundamentals, then learn and adapt.

Good Selling!

Test Your Knowledge

How To Get And Keep Your First Sales Job

1. All entry-level sales positions are the same, so which   True/False
   opportunity you choose will not matter.

2. You can get your career off to a fast start by:
   - a. Deciding on a career path that appeals to you.
   - b. Researching outstanding employers in the field you have chosen.
   - c. Networking.
   - d. Finding a position that fits your Selling Profile.
   - e. All of the above.
   - f. None of the above.

3. Think of a job interview as a_____.

4. Three important interview issues are:

   _____

   _____

   _____

5. Sales Managers need people who can deliver results.   True/False

6. List the five roadblocks to early career success.

   _____

   _____

   _____

   _____

   _____

7. You will prosper in sales if you remember:
   The bottom line in sales is to_____.

APPENDIX A

Index of Illustrations
(In Order of Presentation)

APPENDIX B

Index of Forms
(In Order of Presentation)

INDEX

OTHER BOOKS BY TOM BUTLER

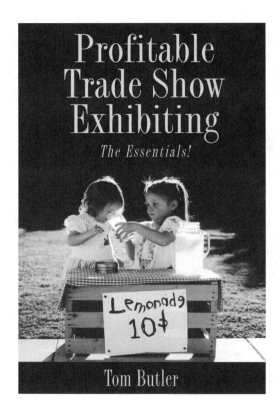

What are the latest trends in today's trade shows? Now there is a remarkable focus on "Show me the money!" Exhibitors are demanding measurable results that impact their bottom line. They want sales and qualified leads! This new conviction extends from basic consumer-oriented shows to large business-to-business events. Trade Shows can positively impact your sales and profits. Learn how to reach this goal through simple, clear and concise actions.

COMING SOON

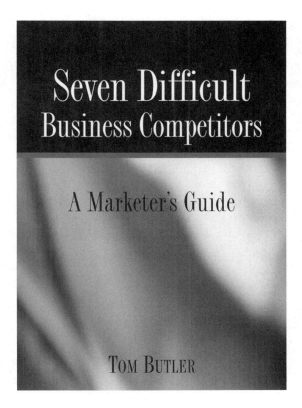

The competition for new and existing customers has never been more intense or of greater importance. Your personal prosperity and the survival of your business are at the very center of this struggle. The ultimate success for each marketer, salesperson, and business owner comes from winning new business from the competition.

We explore the detailed profiles of the seven adversaries facing today's business enterprises, and how you can overcome the challenge each presents. You will learn what attracts potential customers to specific profiles and how to use this to your advantage.

TO ORDER ADDITIONAL TITLES

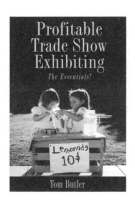

Profitable Trade Show Exhibiting
The Essentials!

$14.99
Paperback
ISBN 0-9718039-8-6

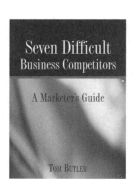

Seven Difficult Business Competitors
A Marketer's Guide

$19.99
Paperback
ISBN 0-9772169-1-8

Available in 2006

Smart Selling

NOTES

Smart Selling

NOTES

Smart Selling

Smart Selling
NOTES

Smart Selling
N O T E S

Smart Selling

NOTES

Smart Selling
NOTES